# *Delicious* DELIGHTS FOR DIABETICS

# *Delicious*
# DELIGHTS
# FOR
# DIABETICS

## DIANNE LOWRY

Illustrations by
Ruth Davey

HODDER AND STOUGHTON
AUCKLAND LONDON SYDNEY TORONTO

*To my husband and special friend Dave.*

Copyright © 1988 Dianne Lowry (text), Ruth Davey (illustrations)
First published 1988
ISBN 0 340 43130X

Typeset by Acorn Graphics Ltd, Auckland.
Printed and bound in Hong Kong for Hodder & Stoughton Ltd, 44-46 View Road, Glenfield, Auckland, New Zealand.

# CONTENTS

Acknowledgements                                          6
Preface                                                   7
Introduction: What is Diabetes?                           9
Food for Diabetics                                       12
Notes on Recipes, Ingredients and Kitchen Equipment      15
Artificial Sweeteners and Their Use                      19

Cool Refreshing Drinks                                   22
Sweet and Savoury Spreads                                30
Scones and Muffins                                       40
Biscuits and Slices                                      49
Loaves                                                   60
Cakes                                                    65
Frozen Delights                                          72
Cool and Light Desserts                                  77
Milk Desserts                                            85
Baked and Steamed Puddings                               91
Custards and Sauces                                      99
Indulgences (Rich Desserts)                             104
Children's Party Ideas                                  117
Cake Decorating: Glazes, Toppings and Fillings          125
Sweets and Treats                                       130
Christmas and Easter Fare                               136
Vegetable Dishes, Salads and Salad Dressings            149

Food Choices Provided by Ingredients                    159
Tips on Modifying 'Non-Diabetic' Recipes                164
Index                                                   171

# ACKNOWLEDGEMENTS

This book would not have become a reality without the encouragement and assistance of many people. Thank you to all who have helped me along the way. In particular:

Joce McDowell for her ideas and enthusiasm

Staff members of the Waikato Diabetic Clinic, especially Sue Scarlet, Dietician, for her invaluable assistance, and Dr Peter Dunn, Endocrinologist, for writing the introduction

Waikato Diabetes Society members for their support

The Biotechnology Division of DSIR for their assistance with the collation of compositional data for New Zealand foods

My family for their forbearance

I would like to advise you of the availability of the following cookbook from the Waikato Diabetes Society, P.O. Box 9382, Hamilton North:

*The Diabetic Cookbook* — Exciting food for everyone
by Vivienne Mason.

# PREFACE

This book is based on personal experience. My husband, Dave, was diagnosed an insulin-dependent diabetic about four years ago. We have both always enjoyed cooking (and, needless to say, eating) and were determined to turn this bad and most unexpected news into positive benefits for our whole family. In retrospect, adapting our family's eating habits to cater for Dave's special needs has heightened rather than dampened our pleasure in the kitchen. Nevertheless there have been problems to overcome.

Initially, there was a feeling of loss associated with having to throw out many tried-and-true recipes enjoyed by the family, especially those familiar recipes you can throw together quickly from memory, when under pressure to produce a meal. In the early days after the diagnosis we had to spend much more time than before planning our meals, searching for and trying new recipes. But with time, we have built up a new reservoir of favourite recipes, and calculating FOOD CHOICES, especially CARBOHYDRATE CHOICES, has become second nature.

When we first began cooking to fit the diet, we experienced an increased food bill, but with greater awareness of what foods and ingredients we really needed to have on hand, gained by personal experience over a few months, our food bill returned to close to our original budget.

Getting acceptable carbohydrate density for the snacks required in Dave's initial daily diet of 3000 Calories proved difficult. I should explain that at the time of diagnosis Dave was involved in marathon running and other such strenuous activities. This is not a problem for overweight diabetics who are generally discouraged from having between-meal snacks, but it is a common hassle for young and energetic diabetics — how to have three to four CARBOHYDRATE CHOICES for morning or afternoon tea without having to munch your way through five to seven cream crackers or the like, plus a piece of fruit (a marathon in itself). We found homemade low-fat, high-carbohydrate baking provided variety and interest and, more importantly, compact servings for snacks.

We have always enjoyed having visitors for meals and going to extra effort when preparing foods for special occasions. To continue to do this we opted to provide only food suitable for diabetics — firstly so that Dave did not have to be treated differently from anyone else at the table, and secondly to save

7

preparation time. Our household is a busy one, and we baulked at the thought of preparing separate dishes for different members of the family if this could be avoided. Obviously the food presented had to be appetising for everybody. This was easy in some areas but difficult in others, for example desserts. But now that we have developed recipes we like, and have become more adept at modifying recipes, this presents no problems at all. Our visitors still keep coming back so we can't be treating them too badly.

Eating out presents little problem at a restaurant (or other eating place) where a choice of fare is provided. Visual assessment of the food on offer, or information provided on the menu (with further clarification from staff if necessary), generally allows suitable selections to be made. Eating at other people's homes can be more difficult. Where possible, to save embarrassment or giving offence, let people know beforehand that you are a diabetic and offer some guidelines as to what foods are and are not appropriate. When invited out for dinner we find it is quite a good ploy to offer to bring the dessert. Taking along a potato or rice dish, or bread, to a pot luck dinner is a good policy to ensure you get the carbohydrate you require.

Each individual diabetic, and his or her family, will face different problems and dilemmas. Solutions that work for us may not be appropriate for you, but we hope you will try, and enjoy, at least some of our recipes. I stress 'our' recipes as Dave has developed many of these recipes and suffered a number of my 'failed' experiments along the way (and vice versa I may add!).

This is not a comprehensive cookbook covering all aspects of meal planning. I have purposely concentrated on providing baking, dessert, beverage, spread and special occasion recipes. We found that applicable recipes in these categories were the hardest to come by. Recipes for suitable vegetable, salad, meat, soup and other savoury dishes can be obtained from many authoritative health cookbooks (for example, those produced by the National Heart Foundation of New Zealand), or from general cookbooks providing care is taken to select low-fat recipes and minimise salt utilisation.

The purpose of this book is simply to demonstrate that you can enjoy a good quality of life with diabetes, in particular, that cooking and eating can still be a pleasure.

Dianne Lowry

# INTRODUCTION:
# WHAT IS DIABETES?

Diabetes mellitus — or more simply diabetes — is a collective term for a group of medical conditions in which blood glucose regulation is impaired or absent. High levels of blood glucose develop which cause symptoms of thirst, urine frequency, dry mouth and cramp and may be associated with recurrent infections and poor wound healing. Weight loss may occur from the excessive loss of glucose in the urine, and from the often faulty and inefficient metabolic processes seen in diabetes.

The causes of diabetes are several, but all produce a partial or total deficiency of insulin secretion. Insulin is a substance made in the pancreas which is released when food is eaten to regulate the increase in blood glucose which would otherwise occur.

There are two main types of diabetes:

Type I — insulin dependent diabetes (IDDM); and

Type II — non-insulin dependent diabetes (NIDDM).

Those people with type I diabetes (IDDM) totally lack insulin production and must take daily insulin injections. This type of diabetes affects less than 0.6% of the population. It is thought to be due to an abnormal response of the immune system to some triggering factor, such as a viral infection, which leads to self-destruction of the cells which make insulin.

The majority of diabetics are type II (NIDDM). For many of these people lifestyle factors are of importance in both the cause and the treatment of their disorder. This type II condition is more common in affluent countries, and is associated particularly with high food intakes, obesity and lack of physical activity. This disorder affects over 3% of all New Zealand adults, more than 6% of those over the age of 50 years, and up to 14% of all adult Maori and Pacific Islands people. Each year over 200 new cases of NIDDM develop in a city the size of Hamilton, over 1000 in Auckland.

Knowledge about food and healthy eating is crucial for diabetics to restore and maintain normal blood glucose levels. It is equally important in the community to reduce the frequency of diabetes. The dietary advice given to diabetics is sound dietary advice for everyone, producing benefits for all — diabetic or not.

For those who are overweight, reduced energy intake is required. Simple weight loss may be all that is needed to restore blood glucose levels to normal in overweight type II diabetics (NIDDM). For both types of diabetes, a major aim of dietary treatment is to remove foods from the diet which cause major increases in blood glucose levels. This means avoiding sugary foods like jam, honey, and soft drinks and cordials sweetened with sugar. Slowly absorbed complex carbohydrate foods, like wholemeal and wholegrain breads and starchy vegetables, are used to reduce swings in blood glucose levels. Increased consumption of complex carbohydrate foods, and reduced consumption of high-protein and high-fat foods is encouraged. High fat intakes, particularly high animal fat intakes, may contribute to elevated blood cholesterol levels — and thus to blood vessel diseases such as coronary artery disease. High protein intakes may cause deleterious affects on the skeleton and will accelerate kidney damage in those with renal disease of any sort.

Diet is not sufficient on its own to manage diabetes, but must be balanced with physical activity, and in some cases drugs — insulin or pills. In insulin-treated diabetics this balancing act is quite difficult and easily upset. It may, if upset, lead to high blood glucose levels with the symptoms mentioned earlier, or cause very low blood glucose levels (a hypoglycaemic attack). The brain is totally dependent on a regular supply of glucose and when the level falls the person afflicted will become irrational and sluggish in their mental and physical processes. Commonly they will experience a racing heart rate, perspiration and hunger. If it is not corrected by taking rapidly absorbed glucose, it may produce coma and convulsions. Here again dietary information and adherence to a diet programme is needed to avoid these dangerous swings in blood glucose. If serious hypoglycaemia does occur, assistance from a family member, friend or work associate may be needed to get the person with a 'hypo' to take glucose tablets or a glucose drink. If they are so groggy that they are unable to swallow these, a doctor must be called urgently. In most families with a diabetic member on insulin treatment, a spouse or parent is shown how to give an intramuscular injection of a hormone — glucagon — for this situation.

Control of blood glucose levels is not only needed to prevent these acute swings in blood glucose, but also to reduce the later onset of 'diabetic complications'. People with diabetes are at greatly increased risk for heart attack, stroke and blockage of leg arteries. Diabetes, especially where poorly controlled, can also lead to eye and kidney diseases. Sustained effort to normalise blood glucose over the life span of the person with diabetes is needed to minimise the risk of these problems. In addition it is now appreciated that it is also important to control the blood levels of the fat cholesterol. Healthy eating is needed to achieve these goals.

In summary, then, diabetes is a distressingly common disorder. Healthy eating patterns are needed not only for the treatment of diabetes, but also throughout the community to reduce the frequency of the more common type II diabetes (NIDDM).

Dr. P.J. Dunn M.D., F.R.A.C.P.,<br>
Endocrinologist, Waikato Diabetic Clinic

# FOOD FOR DIABETICS

The current nutritional recommendations for diabetics are just the same as for all other New Zealanders. For good nutrition everyone should eat:

- large servings of a wide variety of vegetables, and some fresh fruits
- some wholegrain starchy foods, especially wholemeal or wholegrain breads and wholegrain breakfast cereals.
- some milk or other dairy products
- small servings of lean meats, poultry or fish, and some legumes (dried beans, peas and lentils)
- small amounts only of fat and fatty foods, e.g. butter, margarine, fried foods, and high-protein foods like meat and eggs which contain hidden fat
- minimal sugar and sugar-sweetened foods, e.g. soft drinks, confectionery, jams, cordials
- minimal salt and salted foods, e.g. potato chips, salted peanuts, salami
- minimal alcohol and alcoholic drinks
- only enough to maintain weight at right level

However, we do not just eat to be healthy. If we did, food for diabetics would not present any problems, but the reality is that it does. Preparation and consumption of food is an integral part of our life from which we all derive much pleasure and solace. There are many factors — social, economic, religious, ethnic, cultural and so on — which influence what we eat and which extend far beyond nutritional considerations.

A healthy diet offers benefits for everyone, but for a diabetic it is not just desirable, it is imperative for the treatment of diabetes and must be a lifelong commitment.

To balance food intake against exercise activity and their limited insulin production, or insulin regime, diabetics must pay special attention to the *type* and *quantity* of food eaten, and to *when* it is eaten.

Carbohydrate is immensely important in this insulin balancing act. Carbohydrate comes in two forms: simple sugars and complex carbohydrates. Simple sugars include the sugars found in fruit, honey and milk as well as sucrose (table sugar). For diabetics, simple sugars have long been considered the arch-enemy, because eating foods containing significant amounts of these causes rapid increases in blood glucose levels. Recent investigations into the glycaemic responses of various foods (that is the effect that different foods have on blood glucose levels) indicate that this basic supposition is very much an oversimplification. As a greater understanding of carbohydrate assimilation evolves, more emphasis will be placed for diabetics on not eating certain foods in certain situations, rather than the current blacklisting of all foods high in simple sugars. Work done to date indicates that the glycaemic responses to certain foods vary greatly between individuals. If you know, from your own blood glucose testing, that a certain food causes you to have elevated blood glucose levels, then you obviously should avoid that food. Some diabetics find that grapes have this effect, for example.

Moderation in consumption of foods high in simple sugars will always be encouraged for diabetics (irrespective of glycaemic responses) because of their high caloric density. Two teaspoons of sugar provide approximately 10 grams of carbohydrate. To get this amount of carbohydrate from potato you need to eat about one quarter of a cup. It is much more difficult to over-indulge in foods containing complex carbohydrates, especially if those foods are also high in fibre — wholemeal bread, wholegrain cereals, fruits and vegetables, and legumes. We should all eat plenty of these foods. In fact, ideally, at least half our energy intake should be derived from these foods — to reduce our dependency on protein and fatty foods as calorie sources.

While the future offers a ray of hope with possibly more leeway with regard to simple sugar intake, it is now apparent that fat intake is more critical than it was previously thought to be. Diabetics tend to be more prone to heart and vascular disorders than the general public, and a low-fat, low-salt diet is important to minimise the risk of developing such complications. This means cutting down on hidden sources of fat such as occur in high-protein foods (meat, eggs, cheese, nuts, etc.) as well as visible fats like butter, margarine and fat on the outside of meat. Fats have the highest caloric density of all foods — more than double that of foods high in simple sugars!

Fat intake should be low but not nil, as some fat is needed in the diet. This fat intake should ideally be made up of more mono and polyunsaturated fats than saturated fats. To achieve this, fat consumed should come mainly from vegetable and fish, rather than animal sources.

Alcohol affects carbohydrate metabolism and therefore upsets the balancing act done by diabetics between food intake, exercise and insulin regime. We should all moderate our alcohol consumption, but again this is more important for diabetics than non-diabetics. High-sugar alcoholic drinks like beer, sweet wines and sherries, and liqueurs, should be avoided. Dry wines and sherries, and spirits can be consumed in moderation but always *with food*, otherwise alcohol can lower the blood sugar levels dangerously.

It is a sad fact that many diabetics find it difficult to keep to a diet that is appropriate for their condition. A diabetic diet does impose restrictions and the fact that there is no magic cure for diabetes can make it seem like a lifelong sentence. Please do not disregard your diabetes; aim for good blood glucose and weight control. If you are having problems with selecting foods and planning meals to fit your lifestyle, *see your dietitian or doctor for advice*. A diabetic diet can be interesting and appetising, as well as nutritious, for you and your family or flatmates.

# NOTES ON RECIPES, INGREDIENTS AND KITCHEN EQUIPMENT

The recipes in this book have been developed with the nutritional needs of diabetics foremost in mind. In general, sugar, fat and salt have been kept to a minimum and many recipes utilise high-fibre ingredients. However, some treat and special occasion recipes with higher fat content are included. These recipes should not be used frequently.

**Analyses**
For each recipe you will find a list setting out the total energy — expressed as Calories (kcal) and kilojoules (kJ) — along with the weight in grams of carbohydrate, protein, fat and dietary fibre for stated serving sizes. These nutrient values have been calculated using up-to-date food composition tables. Compositional data for New Zealand foods has been used as much as possible. Food composition tables contain averaged analysis figures and can therefore only provide an approximation to the actual nutrient content of the ingredients you use. Calculation figures have been rounded off accordingly. Zero and negligible values have been omitted.

**Food Choices**
FOOD CHOICES are also provided for stated serving sizes. These are based on the FOOD CHOICE Plan as used for diabetics at Waikato Hospital, but can easily be adapted to suit other systems:

I CARBOHYDRATE CHOICE provides approx. I 0g carbohydrate
I PROTEIN CHOICE provides approx. 7g protein, 5g fat
I FAT & OIL CHOICE provides approx. 5g fat

All foods contain a mixture of nutrients, for example a 25g slice of wholegrain bread provides approximately I 0g carbohydrate, 2g protein and I g fat. To keep the FOOD CHOICE Plan as simple as possible, nutrients which provide less than 40% of a FOOD CHOICE per serving are ignored. Hence the 25g slice of wholegrain bread provides I CARBOHYDRATE CHOICE only.

Where variations are given for recipes without additional FOOD CHOICE information, the FOOD CHOICES provided are not significantly different from those provided for the basic recipe.

**Free Foods**
Some recipes are denoted as FREE FOODS, which means that moderate amounts of these foods can be eaten in addition to allowed daily FOOD CHOICES. It is definitely not a rubber stamp for eating excessive quantities of these foods. A FREE FOOD is one which provides less than 4g carbohydrate and 15 kcal (60 kJ) for a normal-sized serving. Most sauces and seasonings come into this category. Hence it is quite acceptable to use conventional recipes (containing added sugar) to make sauces, pickles and chutneys, providing these are used sensibly, in small amounts.

**Low-Calorie Foods**
These provide no more than 8 kcal (35 kJ) per 100ml or 100g.

**High-Fruit Recipes**
In recipes categorised as HIGH FRUIT, carbohydrate from fruit and fruit juice (which is mainly simple sugars), plus any added sugar, make up over 45% of the total carbohydrate present, and the total carbohydrate per serving is 4g or more. To keep intake of simple sugars down it is recommended that diabetics have no more than 2 CARBOHYDRATE CHOICES from fruit and/or HIGH-FRUIT foods at any one meal or snack.

**Dairy-free Recipes**
About half the recipes in this book are denoted as 'dairy free' or 'dairy free if dairy-free margarine used instead of butter'. This is *not* because diabetics should avoid dairy products; they should ideally include some dairy foods in their diet. It is simply that people seeking dairy-free recipes (because of allergy conditions or other reasons), like diabetics, are not very well served for recipes. In baked goods I often use fruit juices in preference to milk because of their greater sweetness (lactose, the sugar in milk, is much less sweet than fruit sugars). Therefore it is often a very simple matter to make these recipes dairy free if desired.

**Measuring**
Careful measuring is essential for consistent cooking results. For the diabetic it is also important to ensure servings provide approximately the FOOD CHOICES required — this applies to both the measuring of ingredients during recipe preparation and the measuring or dividing up of foods into serving-sized portions.
    The recipes in this book are for standard metric measures, lightly

packed (i.e. do not compress ingredients down into measure) and levelled off.

| | | |
|---|---|---|
| 1 level standard metric cup | = | 250 millilitres |
| 1 level standard tablespoon | = | 15 millilitres |
| 1 level standard teaspoon | = | 5 millilitres |

Where gram weights are given, weigh accurately.

**Ingredients**

● All fruit juices are unsweetened.

● All canned or stewed fruit included in recipes must have no added sugar. Use fruit cooked in water or unsweetened fruit juice (with or without arificial sweetener added).

● Use unsalted butter in preference to salted butter. Margarine can be substituted for butter in recipes. If using margarine, select a polyunsaturated low-salt brand.

● Where suitable low-fat alternatives are available these have been used, for example trim milk (non-fat milk with extra non-fat milk solids added to improve body) instead of whole milk; low-fat yoghurt, sour cream and cottage cheese instead of their higher-fat versions; low-fat soft cheese instead of cream cheese. Low-fat cream (a UHT product) is used in some recipes as a cream substitute, but not where whipped cream is needed, because it does not whip.

● No evaporated skim milk is used because the only evaporated milk currently produced in New Zealand is UHT evaporated whole milk. Occasionally, imported evaporated skim milk can be purchased, and this can be used to reduce the fat content of the recipes made with evaporated whole milk. Alternatively, you can make your own. To make the equivalent of 400g of evaporated skim milk (at 20% total solids) mix 80g (approximately ¾ cup) of instant non-fat dried milk with 320ml (approximately 1⅓ cups) water. Disperse thoroughly with a whisk or blender then refrigerate overnight to allow the powder to hydrate.

● Toasted coconut is used in a number of recipes. To toast coconut, heat it in a dry saucepan over medium heat, stirring constantly. Remove coconut from saucepan as soon as it is golden brown, because it quickly burns in the hot saucepan, even if pan is removed from the heat.

## Kitchen Equipment

Diabetics do not need special kitchen equipment but here are a few items which are very handy:

- Plenty of fridge and freezer space
  Reducing the sugar content of foods generally causes the relative humidity to rise, and so too the perishability. This makes refrigerator storage desirable in some cases where it would not normally be required, and essential in others, if wastage is to be avoided. Having freezer space allows more flexibility. For example, I find that freezing muffins and other baked goods so that individual servings can be retrieved easily allows greater variation for lunches and snacks from day to day. Freezer space also allows fruits such as berries to be stored easily (without added sugar) for out-of-season enjoyment. I know people who successfully preserve fruit packed in water, sweetened artificially if necessary, but I personally find freezing fruit much easier (it saves slaving over a boiling pot in the hot summer weather for a start).

- Food Processor
  This is extremely useful for preparing baked goods as well as for chopping and slicing. My cake mixer now sits gathering dust since I have stopped doing baking where the butter and sugar are creamed together. A food processor is a marvellous time saver for rubbing butter or margarine through dry ingredients.

- Steamer
  Steaming vegetables until just cooked allows maximum retention of nutrients during cooking, making a steamer a highly recommended item. Cooking vegetables in a microwave is done essentially by steaming too.

- Stock Separator
  This is an inexpensive plastic measuring jug that has a spout drawing off from the bottom rather than the top. It allows the aqueous part of stock to be separated from the fat component with a minimal amount of fat included — a very desirable function for the fat-conscious cook.

# ARTIFICIAL SWEETENERS AND THEIR USE

In New Zealand there are three types of artificial sweeteners that can be added to foods:

- Saccharin (and its sodium, calcium and ammonium compounds)
- Cyclamate (as either sodium cyclamate or calcium cyclamate)
- Aspartame

The New Zealand Society for the Study of Diabetes makes the following statement regarding artificial sweeteners: 'The use of large amounts of these agents should not be encouraged, but there is little evidence that a low to moderate intake by adults causes harm. With the exception of aspartame, their use by young people and pregnant women should be discouraged.' (''Recommendations for the Nutritional Management of Diabetes Mellitus in New Zealand'' from the Journal of the New Zealand Dietetic Association, October 1986.)

Saccharin and cyclamate are non-nutritive sweeteners. There are liquid forms available of these sweeteners which are quick and easy to use in recipe preparation. Products containing saccharin and/or cyclamate must carry the warning: 'Not recommended for children except on medical advice'.

Aspartame is a nutritive sweetener, but because of its intense sweetness very small amounts are needed to achieve a sweet taste. It does not have the unpleasant after-taste that some people experience with non-nutritive sweeteners, especially saccharin. While artificially produced, aspartame consists of two naturally occurring amino acids, aspartic acid and phenylalanine. Unfortunately, it is only available in New Zealand as a table-top sweetener (in tablets or sachet form). No bulk liquid or powder form is yet available for convenient use in recipe preparation.

Aspartame breaks down to the individual amino acids (and therefore loses its sweetness) when exposed to moisture, especially under acidic conditions. This happens slowly at room and refrigerator temperatures, but rapidly at cooking temperatures. Consequently, it can only be used in recipes that are not cooked, or where the sweetener can be added after cooking.

There is only one aspartame sweetener currently available to domestic consumers in New Zealand — Equal. This contains the Nutrasweet brand of aspartame sweetener that is used in a variety of commerically prepared foods, for example low-calorie soft drinks. Patents for the Nutrasweet brand of aspartame sweetener are running out in New Zealand and more brands of aspartame sweeteners will probably be available in the future.

I avoid using artificial sweeteners wherever possible. Where recipes require the addition of artificial sweetener I have used aspartame, provided it can be added without being subjected to cooking, and if six or fewer sachets give sufficient sweetness (I find using large numbers of sachets very time consuming and inconvenient — you may have more patience). The nutritive value of the aspartame sweetener has been included in the compositional calculations for these recipes. Otherwise I have used a liquid artificial sweetener. The brand I use is Sucaryl artificial sweetening solution, which contains both cyclamate and saccharin. Adopting these rules of thumb for use of sweeteners helps to keep intakes of individual artificial sweetening compounds low. Keep in mind, however, that the use of commercial food preparations containing artificial sweeteners contributes to your total intake of these substances.

Where artificial sweetener is used in recipes, the equivalent amount of sugar is given in brackets to make it easy to substitute one type of sweetener for another.

The following conversion chart was used to arrive at the equivalent quantities of sugar stated:

| Aspartame Sweetener | | Sugar | | Liquid Artificial Sweetener |
|---|---|---|---|---|
| 1 sachet | = | 2 teaspoons | | |
| 2 sachets | = | 4 teaspoons | | |
| 3 sachets | = | 2 tablespoons | = | 1 teaspoon |
| 4 sachets | = | 3 tablespoons | = | 1½ teaspoons |
| 6 sachets | = | ¼ cup | = | 2 teaspoons |
| | | ½ cup | = | 1 tablespoon |
| | | 1 cup | = | 2 tablespoons |

Non-diabetics, please note that I do not guarantee a successful result if recipes are prepared using the stated equivalent amount of sugar instead of sweetener. Where sugar is deleted from recipes, other modifications are often made to compensate for textural changes (see Tips on Modifying 'Non-Diabetic' Recipes, p. 164) — and the same can apply in reverse. The level of sweetness considered desirable in certain foods varies greatly between individuals. This is especially so for the diabetic community — some never loose 'a sweet tooth', while others find that with eating less sweet food their taste preferences shift towards lower sweetness levels. Alter addition rates of artificial sweeteners to suit your own palate.

# COOL REFRESHING DRINKS

When you go out socially, the drinks usually made available are wine, beer, or fruit juice, none of which is ideally suited to the diabetic. The importance of moderating alcohol intake has already been discussed. Unsweetened fruit juices are considered acceptable for diabetics when used in baked goods, but not on their own. In general they contain around 10% simple sugars and provide approximately 40 kcal (170 kJ) per 100ml. Lemon juice is one exception, containing less than 2% sugars and having an energy content of 7 kcal (31 kJ) per 100ml. A cold lemon drink prepared from lemon juice, water and aspartame sweetener is a good thirst quencher that is quite in order. Iced tea and chilled low-calorie mixers are also good. BYO is a good general rule (low-calorie drink — not grog!).

I hope you will find some refreshing ideas for cool drinks amongst the selection of recipes in this section, which includes cordials and other simple drinks for any occasion, smoothie recipes for milkshake maniacs, and mint julep and party punch recipes for entertaining. Most of these drinks have a lemon base (for obvious reasons) and some have added acids. You may notice a loss of sweetness over two to three days in these drinks where aspartame sweetener is used. This is because of its gradual breakdown in acid conditions. Simply add a little more if necessary.

# Lemon Cordial

## Dairy free

This cordial needs a lot of sweetener to balance the tartness of the lemons, hence the use of liquid artificial sweetener rather than aspartame (you could add 24 sachets of aspartame sweetener if you liked!). I do not make this cordial often because of the relatively high amount of liquid artificial sweetener per serving, but I must say I really enjoy this drink.

*grated rind and juice of 2 lemons*
*1 tablespoon tartaric acid*
*1 teaspoon citric acid*
*1 teaspoon Epsom salts*
*2 cups boiling water*
*2 tablespoons liquid artificial sweetener (equivalent to 1 cup sugar)*
*water to dilute*

Place lemon rind and juice, acids and Epsom salts in a bowl. Add boiling water, cover and allow to cool. Transfer to a 2 litre container, add sweetener and then add water to make volume up to 2 litres. Chill. Invert or shake container to ensure cordial is properly mixed before serving (the rind tends to settle to the bottom).

**Makes 2 litres (8 cups)**

**LOW-CALORIE BEVERAGE, FREE FOOD**
**A 180ml serving provides approximately: 2g carbohydrate, 0.1g dietary fibre, 7.5 kcal (32 kJ)**

# Grapefruit Cordial

### Dairy free

Make as for lemon cordial above, replacing the rind and juice of 2 lemons with the rind and juice of 2 grapefruit. Use 6 sachets of aspartame sweetener (equivalent to ¼ cup sugar) instead of liquid artificial sweetener.

*Makes 2 litres (8 cups)*

**LOW-CALORIE BEVERAGE, FREE FOOD**
*A 180ml serving provides approximately: 3.5g carbohydrate, 0.1g protein, 0.2g dietary fibre, 14 kcal (59 kJ)*

# Orange and Lemon Cordial

### Dairy free

*rind and juice of 1 orange*
*rind and juice of 1 lemon*
*1 tablespoon tartaric acid*
*2 cups boiling water*
*6 sachets aspartame sweetener (equivalent to ¼ cup sugar)*
*water to dilute*

Place grated rind and juice of orange and lemon in a bowl. Add tartaric acid and boiling water. Cover and leave to cool. Transfer to a 2 litre container, add sweetener, cap and shake vigorously to dissolve. Add water to make volume up to 2 litres. Chill. Invert

24

container a couple of times before serving to make sure cordial is properly mixed.

*Makes 2 litres (8 cups)*

**LOW-CALORIE BEVERAGE, FREE FOOD**
*A 180ml serving provides approximately: 2.5g carbohydrate, 0.1g protein, 0.2g dietary fibre, 10 kcal (42 kJ))*

# Harvest Drink

**Dairy free**

*¼ cup fine oatmeal*
*½ cup warm water*
*1 lemon, sliced thinly*
*2 litres (8 cups) boiling water*
*6 sachets aspartame sweetener (equivalent to ¼ cup sugar)*

Mix the oatmeal and warm water together in a large bowl. Add the lemon slices, then pour over the boiling water. Cover and leave until cool. Strain through a fine sieve or cloth. Add sweetener and stir to dissolve.

*Makes approximately 1.9 litres (7½ cups)*

*Nutrient values per serving cannot be calculated with any degree of accuracy because of infusion step, but looking at the maximum possible nutrient values this drink definitely qualifies as a **LOW-CALORIE BEVERAGE, FREE FOOD**.*

# King's Cup

**Dairy free**

Fresh basil gives the distinctive flavour to this light and refreshing drink.

*rind of 2 lemons*
*rind of 1 orange*
*6-12 sweet basil leaves, chopped*
*2 sprigs mint, chopped*
*3 cups boiling water*
*juice of 2 lemons*
*juice of 1 orange*
*1½ cups water*
*4 sachets aspartame sweetener (equivalent to 3 tablespoons sugar)*
*sprigs mint or basil for garnish*

Place lemon and orange rind, basil and mint in a large bowl. Pour over the boiling water, cover and leave until cool. Strain out rind and herbs, then add the remaining ingredients. Mix well to ensure sweetener is dissolved. Serve chilled, garnished with sprigs of mint or basil.

*Makes approximately 1.25 litres (5 cups)*

*Nutrient values per serving cannot be calculated with any degree of accuracy because of the infusion step, but looking at the maximum possible nutrient values this drink definitely qualifies as a LOW-CALORIE BEVERAGE, FREE FOOD.*

# Party Punch

**Dairy free**

Fruit punch is generally a 'no-no' for diabetics because of the high fruit juice content — simple sugars and calories abound even if sugar is not added. This recipe contains a relatively small amount of fruit juice compared to normal fruit punch. Lemon and grapefruit juices, which both contain less simple sugars than most fruit juices, make up the bulk of the fruit juice included. Cold tea and ginger ale are used to extend the fruit juice to yield a light, refreshing punch.

2 cups cold tea
⅔ cup lemon juice
⅔ cup grapefruit juice
⅔ cup pineapple juice
1 litre (4 cups) low-calorie ginger ale
ice cubes

First prepare cold tea: make a weak brew of tea and allow to draw for only 2-3 minutes. Strain and chill. Add fruit juices to cold tea. Just before serving add ginger ale (preferably chilled) and ice cubes. Serve with lemon slices and sprigs of mint if desired, or 4-5 strawberries chopped in half. Do not add heaps of fruit, it may look great but it only adds more simple sugars and calories.

*Makes approximately* **2 litres (8 cups)**

**LOW-CALORIE BEVERAGE, FREE FOOD**
A 180ml *serving provides approximately*: 3.5g *carbohydrate*, 0.2g *protein*, 14 *kcal* (61 *kJ*)

27

# Mint Julep

**Dairy free**

*small bunch mint (10-12 leaves)*
*½ cup lemon juice*
*¼ cup water*
*1 litre (4 cups) low-calorie ginger ale*
*ice cubes*

Crush the mint in a bowl. Add lemon juice and water and leave to stand for about half an hour. Strain through a sieve. Add gingerale (preferably chilled) and ice cubes. Serve with sprigs of mint and lemon slices.

*Makes approximately 4¾ cups*

**LOW-CALORIE BEVERAGE, FREE FOOD**
**A 180ml serving provides approximately: 0.5g carbohydrate, 2.5 kcal (11 kJ)**

Here are two smoothie recipes — great for after school or after sport. Blend in 2-3 ice cubes to make thicker smoothies. Serve in tall glasses with bendable straws. (The bendable straw is the most essential ingredient for a good smoothie according to my children!)

# Chocolate Smoothie

*2 cups Trim milk, chilled*
*3 tablespoons unsweetened low-fat natural yoghurt*
*1 tablespoon fine oatmeal*

1 *tablespoon cocoa*
3 *sachets aspartame sweetener (equivalent to 2 tablespoons sugar)*

Place all ingredients into a blender or liquidiser, and blend until smooth. Serve immediately.

*Makes 2 long smoothies*

*Each smoothie provides approximately:*
**2 CARBOHYDRATE CHOICES, 2 PROTEIN CHOICES,**
**19g *carbohydrate*, 13g *protein*, 2g *fat*, 0.3g *dietary fibre*, 150 *kcal* (620 *kJ*)**

# Banana Smoothie

1 *banana*
1½ *cups Trim milk, chilled*
2 *tablespoons unsweetened low-fat natural yoghurt*
1 *teaspoon fine oatmeal*
1 *teaspoon wheatgerm*
1 *sachet aspartame sweetener (equivalent to 2 teaspoons sugar)*

Put banana into blender and blend to mash. Add rest of ingredients, except sweetener and blend until smooth. Check sweetness of smoothie, add and blend in sweetener if required (this depends on the degree of ripeness of the banana used).

*Makes 2 long smoothies*

*Each smoothie provides approximately:*
**2 CARBOHYDRATE CHOICES, 1½ PROTEIN CHOICES,**
**21g *carbohydrate*, 10g *protein*, 1.5g *fat*, 1.5g *dietary fibre*, 130 *kcal* (550 *kJ*)**

# SWEET AND SAVOURY SPREADS

Conventionally made jams and marmalades are high-sugar foods and should only be used very, very sparingly, remembering that 1 teaspoon provides approximately ½ CARBOHYDRATE CHOICE. It is possible to make your own tasty low-carbohydrate sweet spreads using a setting agent.

Agar is used in most of the sweet-spread recipes here. It can be obtained easily from health food shops and gives a more jam-like spreading consistency than can be obtained with gelatine. To use agar successfully it must be boiled to dissolve it. If acid is present when an agar solution is hot the agar will break down. So to make successful agar-set spreads dissolve the agar in a small amount of boiling water and then add this to the cool fruit pulp. The spread will then set in 1-2 hours, or less if the fruit pulp is very cold.

Gelatine can be used in these recipes instead of agar but the spreads take a long time to set with the low addition rates used. Using more gelatine results in a firm jelly texture which does not spread very satisfactorily.

These low-carbohydrate sweet spreads are very perishable and must be stored in the fridge. For this reason the recipe sizes are small.

Savoury spreads are generally higher in fat than sweet spreads. Use these spreads without an underlay of butter or margarine.

If making savouries, use bread cases in preference to pastry cases because they are much lower in fat. Cut out unbuttered bread rounds using a pastry cutter. Push them gently down into ungreased patty pans, then bake at 180°C (350°F) until lightly toasted — about 10 minutes. Fill them with savoury filling, return them to the oven briefly to heat the filling, and serve.

# Lemon Apple Spread

### Dairy free

This has the refreshing lemon flavour of lemon honey without all that unwanted sugar or butter. I enjoy the sharpness of this recipe, but you may prefer it sweeter. If so, add more aspartame sweetener.

*2 eggs, lightly beaten*
*rind and juice of 2 lemons*
*2 medium apples, grated*
*4 sachets aspartame sweetener (equivalent to 3 tablespoons sugar)*

Combine eggs, lemon rind and juice, and grated apple in top half of double boiler. Heat over boiling water, stirring occasionally, until thickened (this takes 5-10 minutes). Remove from heat, add aspartame sweetener and mix through. Pour into jar, and cover. When cool, store in refrigerator, where it will keep for 2-3 weeks.

**Makes approximately 1½ cups**

**Serving size = 1 teaspoon**
**FREE FOOD**
**0.4g carbohydrate, 0.2g protein, 0.2g fat, 0.1g dietary fibre, 4 kcal (16 kJ)**

*Note: The texture of this spread is quite chunky. If you desire a smoother texture, blend the final mix before bottling. To achieve a really smooth texture use ¾ cup unsweetened apple pulp instead of the grated apple.*

# Apricot and Pineapple Spread

**Dairy free**

This unsweetened spread is a personal favourite. It can be used as a shortcake filling too (see recipe p. 106). If you find this too tart for your liking, add some aspartame sweetener to fruit pulp after mashing.

100g dried apricots, chopped
1½ cups water
230g can crushed pineapple in unsweetened pineapple juice, undrained
¼ teaspoon agar (or ½ teaspoon gelatine)
2 tablespoons water

Place apricots, 1½ cups water and crushed pineapple (juice too) in a saucepan. Bring to the boil and simmer gently until apricots are soft (about 20 minutes). Remove from heat and mash to a pulp with a potato masher. Leave to cool. Heat agar (or gelatine) in 2 tablespoons water, stirring continuously, until water boils and agar (or gelatine) dissolves. Add this to cooled apricot and pineapple mix and stir to distribute evenly. Pour into jar(s). Cover and allow to cool and thicken. Store in refrigerator.

---

**Makes approximately 2 cups**

**Serving size = 1 teaspoon**
**FREE FOOD**
**0.8g carbohydrate, 0.1g protein, 0.2g dietary fibre, 3 kcal (14 kJ)**

---

# Date and Orange Spread

## Dairy free

This is another unsweetened spread. Grated apple is added to make the dates go further and help thicken the spread. It, too, can be used as a shortcake filling (see recipe p. 107).

150g dates, chopped
1 cup grated apple, lightly packed (100g)
grated rind of 2 oranges
juice of 2 oranges made up to ½ cup with water
1 cup water
½ teaspoon agar (or 1 teaspoon gelatine)
¼ cup water

Place dates, grated apple, orange rind and juice and 1 cup water in a saucepan. Bring to the boil, cover and simmer gently until the dates are soft (about 20 minutes). Remove from heat and mash to a pulp with a potato masher. Cool until at least tepid. Heat agar (or gelatine) in ¼ cup water until the water boils and the agar (or gelatine) dissolves. Mix this into date and orange pulp. Pour into jar(s). Cover and allow to cool and thicken. Store in refrigerator.

**Makes approximately 2 cups**

**Serving size = 1 teaspoon**
**FREE FOOD**
**1g carbohydrate, 0.2g dietary fibre, 4.5 kcal (20 kJ)**

# Strawberry Spread

## Dairy free

This recipe can be used for other berries too, just adjust the level of sweetness to balance the tartness of the berries used.

200g strawberries (fresh or frozen)
½ cup water
¼ teaspoon agar (or ½ teaspoon gelatine)
3 sachets aspartame sweetener (equivalent to 2 tablespoons sugar)

Place strawberries with ¼ cup water in a saucepan. Bring to the boil and simmer for 15-20 minutes. Remove from heat, break up the strawberries with a fork or potato masher, then cover and leave to cool until lukewarm or cooler. Heat agar (or gelatine) in second ¼ cup water until the water boils and the agar (or gelatine) dissolves. Add this to the strawberry pulp together with the aspartame sweetener. Mix well. Pour into a jar. Cover and leave to set. Store in the refrigerator.

Makes approximately 1 cup

Serving size = 1 teaspoon
FREE FOOD
0.3g carbohydrate, 0.1g dietary fibre, 1.5 kcal (7 kJ)

# Three Fruit Marmalade

## Dairy free

This delicious low-calorie marmalade is made in two steps: first a pulp is prepared, and then the final marmalade is made from a portion of this pulp. Excess pulp can be frozen until required. The reason for this is that without sugar added it does not keep almost indefinitely like genuine marmalade. It is therefore preferable to make relatively small quantities at a time. The final marmalade is very quick to prepare so this is no great inconvenience. The amount of sweetener required to balance the tartness of the citrus fruits is relatively high, hence the use of liquid artificial sweetener rather than aspartame.

## Marmalade Pulp

1 *lemon*
1 *orange*
1 *grapefruit*
2 *cups water (more if required)*

Cut fruit in half and remove pips. Place in a saucepan with 2 cups water. Bring to the boil and simmer gently until flesh of fruit is soft (approximately 30 minutes). Drain off and reserve liquid. Blend softened fruit to a pulp, add reserved liquid and mix (alternatively mash fruit in liquid with a potato masher — fruit needs to be very soft for this). Measure volume of pulp obtained. Add extra water, if necessary, to make volume up to 3¾ cups, and mix well. Freeze in ¾ cup amounts until required.

## Marmalade

¼ *cup water*
¼ *teaspoon agar (or ½ teaspoon gelatine)*
1 *tablespoon liquid artificial sweetener (equivalent to ½ cup sugar)*
¾ *cup marmalade pulp (fresh or thawed from frozen)*

Place water in a saucepan. Sprinkle agar (or gelatine) over the surface, then heat while stirring until water boils and agar (or gelatine) dissolves. Add sweetener and cool marmalade pulp, mix to combine. Pour into jar and cover. Leave to set. Store in refrigerator.

---

*Makes approximately 1 cup*

*Serving size = 1 teaspoon*
**FREE FOOD**
**0.1g carbohydrate, 0.4 kcal (2 kJ)**

---

# Salmon and Egg Spread

This spread can be used as a filling for sandwiches or bread cases. When the weather is cold and miserable this recipe can be served as a hot sauce over toast to help drive away those winter chills.

*25g butter*
*2 tablespoons flour*
*¼ teaspoon salt*
*pepper*
*¾ cup Trim milk*
*210g can salmon, drained and flaked*
*2 tablespoons chopped parsley*
*2 tablespoons chopped chives*
*3 hard-boiled eggs, finely chopped*

Melt butter, then mix in flour, salt and pepper to make a roux. Add milk gradually, stirring until smooth after each addition. Bring to the boil and simmer until thickened, stirring all the time. Remove from heat and mix in balance of ingredients. Serve straight away as a hot sauce, or cool to serve as a spread. Store in refrigerator.

*Makes approximately 2 cups*

**Serving size = 1 teaspoon**
**FREE FOOD**
**0.2g carbohydrate, 0.7g protein, 0.5g fat, 8.5 kcal (35 kJ)**

**Hot sauce serving size = ¼ cup**
**1 PROTEIN CHOICE, ½ FAT & OIL CHOICE,**
**3g carbohydrate, 8.5g protein, 6.5g fat, 0.2g dietary fibre, 110 kcal (440 kJ)**

# Cheese Spread

Use as a sandwich filling, a topping for cheese toast, or best of all as a filling for toasted cheese rolls.

*25g butter*
*½ small onion, finely chopped*
*2 tablespoons flour*
*½ teaspoon prepared mustard*
*1 teaspoon Worcestershire sauce*
*freshly ground black pepper*
*½ cup Trim milk*
*1¼ cups grated tasty Cheddar cheese, lightly packed (100g)*
*2 tablespoons chopped parsley*

Melt butter in small saucepan, add onion and sauté until transparent. Add flour, mustard, Worcestershire sauce, freshly ground black pepper, and stir to form a thick paste. Add milk, and heat while stirring to make a thick, smooth sauce. Remove from heat. Add grated cheese and chopped parsley and mix to combine.

---

**Makes approximately 1 cup**

**Serving size = 1 teaspoon**
**FREE FOOD**
**0.5g carbohydrate, 0.7g protein, 1g fat, 15 kcal (61 kJ)**

*Note: To make Toasted Cheese Rolls: Use a sliced sandwich loaf of wholemeal bread. Remove crusts from slices. Spread top side of each slice with approximately 1½ teaspoons of cheese spread, then roll up with spread inside. Place rolls in oven-proof dish and grill until just golden brown on top, turn and grill again until bottoms too are golden brown. Serve piping hot. Alternatively, these rolls can be baked 15-20 minutes in a moderate oven, but this makes them very crisp and my family think they need butter spread on them if I cook them like this. Grilled lightly on both sides they are perfectly acceptable without any added butter! The recipe above is sufficient to make a loaf of bread into cheese rolls. Freeze any excess rolls uncooked — they are very handy to have on call.*

**1 serving = 1 toasted cheese roll**
**1 CARBOHYDRATE CHOICE,**
**8.5g carbohydrate, 3g protein, 2.5g fat, 1g dietary fibre, 70 kcal (290 kJ)**

---

# Smoked Mussel Pâté

This pâté is simple to make. It can be used as an appetiser with French or crusty wholemeal bread, or just as a change of spread for family meals.

30g butter
2 rashers bacon, finely chopped
½ teaspoon chopped basil
150g low-fat soft cheese
2 tablespoons unsweetened low-fat natural yoghurt
1 tablespoon dry sherry
½ teaspoon Worcestershire sauce
salt and pepper to taste
100g can smoked mussels, drained

Heat butter in pan, add bacon and basil, cook until bacon is tender. Drain. Put bacon and basil into food processor and blend until very fine. Add rest of ingredients except the smoked mussels and blend until smooth. Add smoked mussels and blend just enough to mix through spread. Spoon into serving dish(es). Refrigerate. Try to make this at least 12 hours before serving to allow time for flavours to mingle.

**Makes approximately 1 cup**

**Serving size = 1 teaspoon**
**0.5g carbohydrate, 1g protein, 1g fat, 16 kcal (68 kJ)**
Note: This serving size is just slightly too high in calories to qualify as a free food.

# Chicken Liver Pâté

There are many many different recipes available for chicken liver pâtés. I find this recipe especially enticing — the inclusion of green peppercorns is the master stroke.

¼ cup celery tops
6 black peppercorns
1 bay leaf
3 cups water
250g chicken livers
50g butter
1 clove garlic, crushed
¼ cup finely chopped onion
½ teaspoon thyme
1 tablespoon brandy
¼ teaspoon salt
¼ teaspoon ground allspice
3 teaspoons green peppercorns, drained and rinsed
2 tablespoons cream

Place celery tops, black peppercorns, and bay leaf in a saucepan with water. Bring to the boil, then simmer for 10 minutes. Add chicken livers and simmer them gently in this stock for 10 minutes. Remove from heat and drain stock off livers. The livers should still be slightly pink inside.

While stock is simmering, melt butter in a frying pan, add garlic, onion and thyme, cover and cook over medium heat until onion is almost transparent. Place this mixture in food processor. Add poached chicken livers, brandy, salt, allspice and green peppercorns. Blend until very smooth. Add cream and blend to combine.

Transfer mixture into pate pots, cover and refrigerate. For best flavour leave overnight for individual flavours to mingle, and allow pate to stand at room temperature for about half an hour before serving. Serve with wholegrain toast or French bread (unbuttered).

---

**Makes approximately 1 cup**

**Serving size = 1 teaspoon**
**0.2g carbohydrate, 0.9g protein, 1.5g fat, 17 kcal (69 kJ)**

Note: This serving size is just slightly too high in calories to qualify as a
FREE FOOD.

---

# SCONES AND MUFFINS

These are quick to make and always popular. Mix the dry ingredients together with a fork, before adding any fruit or liquid ingredients, to incorporate air. Mix all the liquid ingredients into the dry ingredients in one step and do not overmix — especially with muffins. If practical, use ingredients at room temperature rather than chilled. I find that scones turn out best if the dough is almost too sticky to handle.

The sizes of some of the scones may seem small, especially for recipes including dried fruit. This is to keep the number of CARBOHYDRATE CHOICES per scone to 2 or less if practical.

# Savoury Scones

These always go down well — for lunch, morning or afternoon tea, supper, or with a barbeque tea. This recipe can be readily adapted to use whatever ingredients you have on hand. Bacon chips, chopped spring onion or chives, Parmesan cheese or crushed garlic could be used instead of tomato or parsley.

2 cups flour
3 teaspoons baking powder
pinch cayenne pepper
½ cup (40g) grated tasty Cheddar cheese
½ small onion, finely grated
1 small tomato, finely diced
1 tablespoon chopped parsley
¾ cup Trim milk (approximately)

Place flour, baking powder and cayenne pepper in a bowl and mix. Add cheese, onion, tomato and parsley and mix. Make a well in the centre of the dry ingredients and pour milk into this. Mix to form a soft dough, adding a little more milk if necessary to give the desired consistency. Turn dough on to a lightly floured surface. Lightly flour your fingers and knead the dough a little. Shape dough into a rectangle and cut into 12 scones (or 8 if you prefer large farmhouse scones). Transfer to a greased oven tray and bake 12-15 minutes at 200°C (400°F).

Makes 12 scones
1 serving = 1 scone
2 CARBOHYDRATE CHOICES, ½ PROTEIN CHOICE,
19g carbohydrate, 4.5g protein, 1.5g fat, 1.5g dietary fibre, 110 kcal (450 kJ)

Alternatively, makes 8 large farmhouse scones
1 serving = ½ scone
1½ CARBOHYDRATE CHOICES, ½ PROTEIN CHOICE,
14g carbohydrate, 3.5g protein, 1g fat, 1g dietary fibre, 80 kcal (340 kJ)

# Date and Wheatgerm Scones

**Dairy free if dairy-free margarine used instead of butter**

These are delicious with lemon apple spread (see recipe p. 31) or with date and orange spread (see recipe p. 33).

½ *cup wholemeal flour*
½ *cup flour*
½ *cup wheatgerm*
2 *teaspoons baking powder*
1 *tablespoon butter*
⅓ *cup chopped dates*
½ *cup unsweetened apple juice (approximately)*

Place flours, wheatgerm, baking powder and butter in a mixing bowl, then rub the butter through the dry ingredients until the mix resembles fine breadcrumbs (you could do this in a blender but I find with this small amount of butter it is not worth the effort of cleaning the blender afterwards). Mix in the chopped dates, make a well in the centre of the dry ingredients and pour apple juice into this. Mix to form a sticky dough, adding a little more apple juice if necessary to give the desired consistency. Turn dough on to a lightly floured surface and shape into an oblong with lightly floured fingers. Cut into 8 scones. Transfer to a greased oven tray and bake 12-15 minutes at 200ºC (400ºF).

*Makes 8 scones*

1 *serving* = 1 *scone*
2 CARBOHYDRATE CHOICES, ½ PROTEIN CHOICE,
21g *carbohydrate,* 3g *protein,* 2g *fat,* 2g *dietary fibre,* 120 *kcal* (490 *kJ*)

# Spicy Sultana and Apricot Scones

**Dairy free if dairy-free margarine used instead of butter**

Serve with apricot and pineapple spread (p. 32) for a mouth-watering treat.

¾ *cup wholemeal flour*
¾ *cup flour*
2 *teaspoons baking powder*
1 *teaspoon cinnamon*
½ *teaspoon mixed spice*
1 *tablespoon butter*
¼ *cup sultanas*
3 *dried apricots, finely chopped*
½ *cup unsweetened apple juice (approximately)*

Place flours, baking powder, spices and butter in a mixing bowl, then rub the butter through the dry ingredients until the mix resembles fine breadcrumbs. Mix in the sultanas and chopped apricots, make a well in the centre of the dry ingredients and pour apple juice into this. Mix to form a sticky dough, adding a little more apple juice if necessary to give the desired consistency. Turn dough on to a lightly floured surface and shape into an oblong with lightly floured fingers. Cut into 8 scones. Transfer to a greased oven tray and bake 12-15 minutes at 200ºC (400ºF).

**Makes 8 scones**

**1 *serving* = 1 *scone***
**2½ CARBOHYDRATE CHOICES, ½ PROTEIN CHOICE,**
**25g *carbohydrate*, 3.5g *protein*, 2g *fat*, 3g *dietary fibre*, 130 *kcal***
**(550 kJ)**

Note: *To reduce the CARBOHYDRATE CHOICES per scone down to 2, this recipe would have to be made into 10 scones which would be ridiculously small. Do keep tabs on how many you have eaten because for their size they really are high in carbohydrate.*

# Herb Pumpkin Damper

**Dairy free if dairy-free margarine used instead of butter**

For this recipe use old crown pumpkin rather than soft varieties like butternut, and do not add any butter or milk to the pumpkin when you mash it. You will need about 500g raw pumpkin to yield a cup of mashed pumpkin.

1 cup flour
¾ cup wholemeal flour
3 teaspoons baking powder
25g butter
1 cup mashed pumpkin
½ small onion, grated
1 clove garlic, crushed (optional)
2 tablespoons chopped parsley
2 tablespoons chopped chives
¼ teaspoon chicken stock powder
freshly ground black pepper
2 tablespoons water

Place flour, wholemeal flour, baking powder and butter in a food processor and blend until the butter is rubbed through the dry ingredients. Add all the remaining ingredients and blend until combined. Spoon all the dough into a heap on a greased oven tray. With lightly floured fingers shape dough into a circle approximately 15 cm in diameter. Mark top with a cross. Bake 10 minutes at 200ºC (400ºF) then a further 20 minutes at 180ºC (350ºF).

*Makes 1 damper*

*Divided into 10 equal servings, each serving provides approximately:*
**2 CARBOHYDRATE CHOICES, ½ PROTEIN CHOICE,**
**19g carbohydrate, 3.5g protein, 2.5g fat, 2g dietary fibre, 110 kcal (480 kJ)**

# Fruity Muffins

**Dairy free if dairy-free margarine used instead of butter**

A versatile recipe that can be used to make a variety of fruity muffins. Substitute the crushed pineapple with 1 cup of pulped apple, peach or apricot prepared from canned or stewed fruit (drained first if packed in reasonable amount of liquid). Check sweetness of fruit pulp used. These muffins are quite sweet enough when made with pineapple, but could need some liquid artificial sweetener added when prepared using a different fruit base. For best results use fruit at room temperature — not chilled.

¾ *cup wholemeal flour*
½ *cup flour*
2 *teaspoons mixed spice*
1 *teaspoon bicarbonate of soda*
½ *cup sultanas*
1 *egg*
230g *can crushed pineapple, undrained*
50g *butter, melted*

Put flours, mixed spice and bicarbonate of soda into a mixing bowl. Mix with a fork to incorporate air. Mix in sultanas, then form a well in the centre of these dry ingredients. In a separate bowl, lightly beat egg, then mix in crushed pineapple (or fruit of choice plus sweetener if necessary) and melted butter. Pour these liquid ingredients into well in dry ingredients, then mix with a fork until just combined (do not overmix). Spoon mixture evenly into 12 greased muffin pans. Bake 10-15 minutes at 200°C (400°F).

*Makes* **12** *muffins*

1 *serving* = 1 *muffin*
1½ CARBOHYDRATE CHOICES, 1 FAT & OIL CHOICE,
**17g** *carbohydrate,* **2.5g** *protein,* **4g** *fat,* **2g** *dietary fibre,* **120** *kcal*
**(490** *kJ***)**

# Courgette and Carrot Muffins

**Dairy free if dairy-free margarine used instead of butter**

2½ *cups wholemeal flour*
1½ *teaspoons baking powder*
½ *teaspoon bicarbonate of soda*
1 *teaspoon cinnamon*
½ *cup raisins*
¼ *cup walnuts, chopped*
1 *cup grated carrot, lightly packed*
1 *cup grated courgette, lightly packed*
2 *eggs*
1 *cup unsweetened apple juice*
50g *butter, melted*

Measure dry ingredients into a bowl and mix together with a fork. Mix in carrot and courgette. In a separate bowl, lightly beat eggs and apple juice together. Pour egg mix and melted butter into a well in dry ingredients, then mix with a fork until just combined (do not overmix). Spoon equal amounts into 15 greased muffin pans. Bake 15-20 minutes at 200°C (400°F).

*Makes 15 muffins*

1 *serving* = 1 *muffin*
2 CARBOHYDRATE CHOICES, ½ PROTEIN CHOICE, ½ FAT &
OIL CHOICE,
22g *carbohydrate, 4.5g protein, 5g fat, 3g dietary fibre, 150 kcal
(620 kJ)*

# Peaches and Cream Muffins

Lovely light muffins filled with a low-calorie cream.

## Muffins

1 cup wholemeal flour
1 cup flour
1½ teaspoons baking powder
1 teaspoon bicarbonate of soda
1 teaspoon cinnamon
¼ teaspoon nutmeg
425g can peaches in unsweetened fruit juice
2 eggs
2 teaspoons liquid artificial sweetener (equivalent to ¼ cup sugar)
½ cup low-fat sour cream

## Filling

½ cup low-fat sour cream
3 tablespoons peach puree (put aside when making muffins — see method below)
1 sachet aspartame sweetener (equivalent to 2 teaspoons sugar)
¼ teaspoon vanilla essence

Mix flours, baking powder, bicarbonate of soda and spices together in a bowl, then form a well in the centre of these ingredients. Puree peaches (undrained) in blender. Put aside 3 tablespoons of this puree for filling. Add eggs, sweetener and sour cream to peach puree in blender and blend to combine. Pour this mixture into a well in dry ingredients, then mix with a fork just enough to combine (do not overmix). Divide mixture evenly between 15 greased muffin pans. Bake 15-20 minutes at 200ºC (400ºF).

Mix all filling ingredients together, then refrigerate until muffins are cool. Make a diagonal slit in each muffin and fill with a good heaped teaspoon of filling.

---

*Makes 15 filled muffins*

1 *serving* = 1 *filled muffin*
2 CARBOHYDRATE CHOICES, ½ PROTEIN CHOICE,
18g *carbohydrate*, 4.5g *protein*, 3g *fat*, 1.5g *dietary fibre*, 120 *kcal*
(490 *kJ*)

---

# Curry Beansprout Muffins

## Dairy free

Try these tasty muffins for a change. The salt included in the recipe is needed for flavour.

*1 cup wholemeal flour*
*1 cup flour*
*1½ teaspoons baking powder*
*1 teaspoon bicarbonate of soda*
*1 teaspoon curry powder*
*¼ teaspoon salt (or to taste)*
*freshly ground black pepper*
*1½ cups (65g) alfalfa beansprouts*
*3 tablespoons chopped chives*
*2 eggs*
*¾ cup water*
*¼ cup vegetable oil*

Place flours, baking powder, bicarbonate of soda, curry powder, salt and pepper in a large bowl and mix. Add beansprouts and chopped chives and mix through, then form a well in the centre. In a separate bowl, beat the eggs, water and oil together until thick and frothy. Pour the egg mixture into the well in the dry ingredients, then mix with a fork just enough to combine all the ingredients (do not overmix). Divide mixture evenly between 12 greased muffin pans. Bake 15-20 minutes at 200ºC (400ºF).

*Makes 12 muffins*

*1 serving = 1 muffin*
1½ CARBOHYDRATE CHOICES, ½ PROTEIN CHOICE, ½ FAT & OIL CHOICE,
*17g carbohydrate, 4.5g protein, 6g fat, 2g dietary fibre, 140 kcal (580 kJ)*

# BISCUITS AND SLICES

Biscuits rely on sugar for crispness, and on fat for shortness. It is difficult, if not impossible, to get an acceptable texture with low sugar and low fat levels. Liquid artificial sweetener generally has to be added because there is very little scope for using fruit juices for sweetening (very little liquid is added to biscuit mixes).

The biscuit recipes included in this section have a small amount of sugar added to give a little crispness. The ratio of fat to carbohydrate is higher than for other types of baking recipes. For these reasons, I do not make biscuits often, preferring to make slices, cakes or loaves.

Slices have traditionally been baked in sponge roll tins in New Zealand family homes. It takes quite a large recipe to fill a sponge-roll tin; this might be fine for a family with growing children but is less practical for smaller households. For this reason half-recipes are given, as well as full recipes for sponge-roll tins.

# Spice Biscuits

**Dairy free if dairy-free margarine used instead of butter**

¾ cup flour
½ cup ground rice
1 teaspoon baking powder
2 tablespoons brown sugar
1 teaspoon cinnamon
1 teaspoon mixed spice
1 teaspoon ground ginger
75g butter
1 egg
2 teaspoons liquid artificial sweetener (equivalent to ¼ cup sugar)

Place all the dry ingredients and the butter into a food processor and blend until mixture resembles fine crumbs. Add egg and artificial sweetener and blend until mixture forms crumbly dough. Press dough into a large ball with fingers. Pinch off small pieces of dough, form into balls, place on oven tray and flatten with a fork (or roll dough out to 0.5cm thick and cut biscuit shapes of your choice). Bake 15-20 minutes at 180ºC (350ºF).

*Makes 20 biscuits*

**1 serving = 1 biscuit**
**1 CARBOHYDRATE CHOICE, ½ FAT & OIL CHOICE,**
**8g carbohydrate, 1.5g protein, 3.5g fat, 0.6g dietary fibre, 69 kcal (290 kJ)**

# Rolled Oat and Coconut Biscuits

**Dairy free if dairy-free margarine used instead of butter**

These are an adaptation of Anzac biscuits — unfortunately not as crisp, but very tasty none the less.

¾ *cup wholemeal flour*
½ *cup ground rice*
1 *cup coconut*
1 *cup rolled oats*
75g *butter*
2 *tablespoons golden syrup*
½ *teaspoon bicarbonate of soda*
⅓ *cup near-boiling water*
2 *teaspoons liquid artificial sweetener (equivalent to* ¼ *cup sugar)*

Place wholemeal flour, ground rice, coconut and rolled oats in a bowl and mix. Melt together butter and golden syrup. Dissolve bicarbonate of soda in near-boiling water and add this to butter and golden syrup. Make a well in centre of dry ingredients and pour into it the prepared liquid mix and the artificial sweetener. Mix well. Pinch off small pieces of dough, roll into balls, place on oven tray and flatten with a fork. Bake 15-20 minutes at 180ºC (350ºF).

*Makes* **20 biscuits**

1 *serving* = 1 *biscuit*
1 CARBOHYDRATE CHOICE, 1 FAT & OIL CHOICE,
12g *carbohydrate, 1.5g protein, 5.5g fat, 1.5g dietary fibre,* 100 *kcal*
(430 *kJ*)

# Peanut Brownies

**Dairy free if dairy-free margarine used instead of butter**

I tend not to make these very often because they seem to disappear very quickly — too quickly for the cook's liking!

¾ cup wholemeal flour
½ cup ground rice
2 tablespoons sugar
1 tablespoon cocoa
1 teaspoon baking powder
75g butter
1 egg
2 teaspoons liquid artificial sweetener (equivalent to ¼ cup sugar)
2 tablespoons water
1 cup peanuts

Place wholemeal flour, ground rice, sugar, cocoa, baking powder and butter in a food processor and blend until the mix resembles fine crumbs. Add egg, sweetener and water, then blend again until mixed well. Finally add peanuts and mix through dough. Using fingers, take small chunks of mixture, press together, roll roughly into balls and place on greased oven tray. Flatten balls with moistened fingertips. Bake 15-20 minutes at 180ºC (350ºF).

**Makes 20 biscuits**

*1 serving = 1 biscuit*
**1 CARBOHYDRATE CHOICE, ½ PROTEIN CHOICE, 1 FAT &
OIL CHOICE,**
*9g carbohydrate, 3g protein, 7.5g fat, 1g dietary fibre, 120 kcal
(480 kJ)*

# Shortbread Triangles

**Dairy free if dairy-free margarine used instead of butter**

Not as short as real shortbread made with heaps of butter and
icing sugar (and no egg), but quite acceptable and much less
calorific! I find the clean taste of shortbread makes the bitter
aftertaste of liquid artificial sweetener more noticeable than usual,
so I add only a small amount. Using the specified amount of icing
sugar with no added sweetener gives a slight sweetness, but not
quite enough for my liking. However, increasing the amount of
icing sugar added would step over that discretionary line of what
is considered acceptable with regard to added sugar in recipes
for diabetics.

¾ *cup flour*
½ *cup cornflour*
2 *tablespoons icing sugar*
1 *teaspoon baking powder*
75g *butter*
1 *egg*
1 *teaspoon liquid artificial sweetener (equivalent to 2 tablespoons sugar)*

Place flour, cornflour, icing sugar, baking powder and butter in
a food processor and blend until the butter is rubbed through
the dry ingredients. Add egg and sweetener, and blend until dough
forms. Divide mixture in half and roll each half out to a circle
approximately 20 cm in diameter. Transfer both circles to an oven
tray. Use your fingers to pinch around the outside of each circle
to give a fluted edge. Cut each circle into 8 equal segments. Bake
at 180°C (350°F) until cooked, approximately 15 minutes.

*Makes* 16 *triangles*

1 *serving* = 1 *triangle*
1 CARBOHYDRATE CHOICE, 1 FAT & OIL CHOICE,
10g *carbohydrate,* 1.5g *protein,* 4.5g *fat,* 0.4g *dietary fibre,* 84 *kcal*
(350 *kJ*)

# Dusky Dandy

A tasty slice which is very popular in our household.

**Half recipe**
50g butter
½ cup coconut, toasted
1 cup sultanas
½ cup flour
½ cup wholemeal flour
1 teaspoon baking powder
1 tablespoon cocoa
1 tablespoon liquid artifical sweetener (equivalent to ½ cup sugar)
¼ cup Trim milk
½ teaspoon vanilla essence
1 egg

**Full recipe**
100g butter
1 cup coconut, toasted
2 cups sultanas
1 cup flour
1 cup wholemeal flour
2 teaspoons baking powder
2 tablespoons cocoa
2 tablespoons liquid artificial sweetener (equivalent to 1 cup sugar)
½ cup Trim milk
1 teaspoon vanilla essence
2 eggs

Melt butter in a large saucepan. Remove from heat, add all the rest of the ingredients and mix to a stiff dough. Press half recipe evenly over base of greased 15 x 20cm cake tin, or full recipe over base of greased sponge-roll tin. Bake 20-25 minutes at 180ºC (350ºF). While still warm, cut half recipe into 12 fingers, or full recipe into 24 fingers.

*Half recipe makes* 12 *fingers, full recipe makes* 24 *fingers*

1 *serving* = 1 *finger*
1½ **CARBOHYDRATE CHOICES, 1 FAT & OIL CHOICE,**
17*g carbohydrate,* 2.5*g protein,* 6*g fat,* 2.5*g dietary fibre,* 130 *kcal*
**(560 k])**

**HIGH-FRUIT RECIPE**

# Carob Orange Square

**Dairy free if dairy-free margarine used instead of butter**

This recipe is similar to the Dusky Dandy recipe but the flavour is quite different. The use of carob instead of cocoa, and orange juice instead of milk, makes the addition of artificial sweetener unnecessary.

### Half recipe
50g butter
½ cup coconut
1 cup wholemeal flour
1 tablespoon carob powder
1 teaspoon baking powder
1 cup sultanas
grated rind of ½ orange
juice of 1 orange made up to ¼ cup with water
1 egg

### Full recipe
100g butter
1 cup coconut
2 cups wholemeal flour
2 tablespoons carob powder
2 teaspoons baking powder
2 cups sultanas
grated rind of 1 orange
juice of 2 oranges made up to ½ cup with water
2 eggs

Melt butter in a large saucepan. Remove from heat, add all the rest of the ingredients and mix to a stiff dough. Press half recipe evenly into a greased 15 x 20cm cake tin, or full recipe into a greased sponge-roll tin. Bake 20-25 minutes at 180°C (350°F). Cut half recipe into 12 squares, or full recipe into 24 squares, while still warm.

*Half recipe makes 12 squares, full recipe makes 24 squares*

1 *serving* = 1 *square*
2 CARBOHYDRATE CHOICES, 1 FAT & OIL CHOICE,
*18g carbohydrate, 2.5g protein, 6g fat, 3g dietary fibre, 130 kcal (550 kJ)*

HIGH-FRUIT RECIPE

# Apple and Honey Slice

**Dairy free if dairy-free margarine used instead of butter**

The small amount of honey included gives this slice its distinctive flavour.

## Half recipe
50g butter
1 tablespoon honey
½ cup grated apple, lightly packed (50g)
¾ cup wholemeal flour
½ teaspoon baking powder
½ teaspoon cinnamon
½ teaspoon mixed spice
¼ teaspoon nutmeg
¾ cup sultanas
¼ cup chopped walnuts
1 egg

## Full recipe
100g butter
2 tablespoons honey
1 cup grated apple, lightly packed (100g)
1½ cups wholemeal flour
1 teaspoon baking powder
1 teaspoon cinnamon
1 teaspoon mixed spice
½ teaspoon nutmeg
1½ cups sultanas
½ cup chopped walnuts
2 eggs

Melt butter and honey together in a large saucepan. Remove from heat, add all the other ingredients and mix well to combine. Spread half recipe evenly into a greased 15 x 20cm cake tin, or full recipe into a greased sponge-roll tin. Bake 20-25 minutes at 160ºC (325ºF). Cut half recipe into 12 squares or full recipe into 24 squares.

*Half recipe makes* 12 *squares, full recipe makes* 24 *squares*

1 *serving* = 1 *square*
1½ CARBOHYDRATE CHOICES, 1 FAT & OIL CHOICE,
14g *carbohydrate,* 2g *protein,* 5g *fat,* 2g *dietary fibre,* 110 *kcal*
(460 *kJ*)

HIGH-FRUIT RECIPE

# LOAVES

These recipes are very low in fat, so take care to prepare baking tins adequately. Line the base of the tin with greaseproof paper, then grease this paper. After baking, run a knife around the edges of the tin to loosen the sides of loaf from the tin. Shake the tin gently to ensure the bottom of the loaf is free. Turn the loaf out and remove the greaseproof paper before the loaf has cooled appreciably.

The loaf recipes generally say to slice them into 20 slices. These slices are thin. If you find it difficult to slice a loaf this thinly, cut it into 10 chunky slices and cut these down the middle. This gives more cake-like servings, which people are less inclined to butter. Remember, too, if you get 18 or 19 servings instead of 20 out of a loaf, this only represents a 5-10% error in the FOOD CHOICES calculated, which does not matter particularly.

# Banana Yoghurt Loaf

A moist and tasty loaf. Use very ripe bananas to give as much natural sweetness to the loaf as possible.

¼ cup (25g) walnut pieces
1 cup wholemeal flour
½ cup flour
1 teaspoon baking powder
1 teaspoon bicarbonate of soda
50g butter
½ cup rolled oats
2 large ripe bananas, mashed (should yield about 1 cup)
½ cup unsweetened low-fat natural yoghurt
2 tablespoons honey

Place walnut pieces in blender and blend until chopped finely. Add flours, baking powder, bicarbonate of soda and butter to blender. Blend to rub butter through dry ingredients. Add rolled oats, mashed banana, yoghurt and honey, and blend to mix thoroughly. Transfer loaf mixture to a prepared (base lined with greaseproof paper and greased) small bread tin. Make a hollow in the centre of the mixture with the back of a spoon. Bake at 160°C (325°F) until cooked, approximately 45-60 minutes.

**Makes 1 loaf**

**Divided into 20 equal slices, each slice provides approximately:**
**1½ CARBOHYDRATE CHOICES, ½ FAT & OIL CHOICE,**
**13g carbohydrate, 2g protein, 3g fat, 1.5g dietary fibre, 90 kcal (370 kJ)**

# Banana, Orange and Coconut Loaf

**Dairy free if dairy-free margarine used instead of butter**

This is a must for coconut lovers.

1 cup flour
½ cup wholemeal flour
1 teaspoon baking powder
1 teaspoon bicarbonate of soda
50g butter
½ cup coconut, toasted
1 ripe banana, mashed (should yield about ⅓ cup)
grated rind of 1 orange
juice of 1 orange made up to ⅓ cup with water
2 teaspoons liquid artificial sweetener (equivalent to ¼ cup sugar)
1 egg

Place flours, baking powder, bicarbonate of soda and butter in a food processor and blend until butter rubbed through the dry ingredients. Add all the rest of the ingredients and blend to mix. Transfer mix to a prepared (base lined with greaseproof and greased) 10 x 20cm loaf tin. Cook 40-50 minutes at 160ºC (325ºF).

---

**Makes 1 loaf**

**Divided into 20 equal slices, each slice provides approximately:
1 CARBOHYDRATE CHOICE, ½ FAT & OIL CHOICE,
9g carbohydrate, 2g protein, 3.5g fat, 1.5g dietary fibre, 75 kcal (310 kJ)**

---

# Fruit and Tea Loaf

## Dairy free

A delicious moist loaf, which is quick to prepare, and best of all has no added fat.

*½ cup each raisins, sultanas and currants*
*1 tablespoon dry sherry or brandy*
*1 teaspoon bicarbonate of soda*
*½ cup freshly brewed tea, strained*
*1 cup wholemeal flour*
*1 egg*

Place dried fruit in a bowl. Pour over sherry (or brandy). Dissolve bicarbonate of soda in tea and pour over fruit. Break up any clumps of fruit with a spoon, then add flour and egg, and mix until all ingredients are combined. Transfer mixture into a prepared (base lined with greaseproof paper and greased) 10 x 20cm loaf tin. Bake 25-30 minutes at 160°C (325°F).

**Makes 1 loaf**

**Divided into 20 equal slices, each slice provides approximately:**
**1 CARBOHYDRATE CHOICE,**
**12g carbohydrate, 1.5g protein, 0.4g fat, 1.5g dietary fibre, 56 kcal (240 kJ)**

**HIGH-FRUIT RECIPE**

# Gingerbread Loaf

This is a very spicy loaf. If you do not like too much spice, reduce the amounts of ginger and cinnamon added.

*2 cups wholemeal flour*
*1 tablespoon ground ginger*
*1 tablespoon cinnamon*
*1½ teaspoons bicarbonate of soda*
*25g butter*
*2 eggs*
*2 tablespoons golden syrup*
*¾ cup unsweetened low-fat natural yoghurt*
*½ cup sultanas*

Place flour, spices, bicarbonate of soda and butter in a food processor. Blend until butter rubbed through dry ingredients. Add all the remaining ingredients and blend until mixed thoroughly. Transfer mixture to a prepared (base lined with greaseproof paper and greased) small bread tin. Hollow out centre of mixture with the back of a spoon, then bake at 160ºC (325ºF) until cooked, approximately 45-60 minutes.

**Makes 1 loaf**

**Divided into 20 equal slices, each slice provides approximately:**
**1½ CARBOHYDRATE CHOICES, ½ PROTEIN CHOICE,**
**15g carbohydrate, 3g protein, 2g fat, 1.5g dietary fibre, 88 kcal (370 kJ)**

# CAKES

As for loaves, take care with the preparation of the baking tins. Remove the cake from the tin and remove the greaseproof paper from the bottom of the cake while it is still warm. The 'high-fruit' cakes keep better than other diabetic cakes because of the higher sugar content. They do not, however, keep virtually indefinitely like a conventional rich fruit cake made with sugar.

The fruit cake recipes included are purposely made fairly shallow to facilitate cutting into small serving sizes. The deeper the cake, the more difficult this is.

Fruit cakes are best cooked slowly at low heat. If you have a conventional electric oven (there is no need to do this with a thermowave) place a thin section of newspaper folded in half on the rack under the cake tin. Place another rack just above the cake with another section of newspaper folded in half on it. These slow the heat penetration. Remove the upper newpaper a little before the end of the cooking time to allow the top of the cake to brown. Do *not* put newspaper in a gas oven, and wait until your electric oven has reached the desired cooking temperature before you put the newpaper in.

See the chapter on cake decorating ideas for glaze and filling recipes.

# Wholemeal Banana Cake

**Dairy free if dairy-free margarine used instead of butter**

1½ cups wholemeal flour
½ cup wheatgerm
3 teaspoons baking powder
75g butter
2 large very ripe bananas, mashed (should yield about 1 cup)
3 eggs
1 tablespoon liquid artificial sweetener (equivalent to ½ cup sugar)
½ cup water

Place wholemeal flour, wheatgerm, baking powder and butter in a food processor and blend until butter rubbed through dry ingredients. Add mashed bananas, eggs, sweetener and water. Blend to combine. Transfer cake mixture into prepared (base lined with greaseproof paper and greased) ring tin, and spread out evenly. Bake 35 minutes at 160°C (325°F). Once cool, store in refrigerator.

*Makes 1 cake*

**Divided into 20 equal servings, each serving provides approximately:**
**1 CARBOHYDRATE CHOICE, ½ PROTEIN CHOICE, ½ FAT &**
**OIL CHOICE,**
*11g carbohydrate, 3g protein, 4.5g fat, 1.5g dietary fibre, 93 kcal*
*(390 kJ)*

# Chocolate Cake

1 cup wholemeal flour
1 cup flour
¼ cup cocoa
3 teaspoons baking powder
50g butter
3 eggs
1 tablespoon liquid artificial sweetener (equivalent to ½ cup sugar)
1 tablespoon dry sherry
¾ cup unsweetened low-fat natural yoghurt
½ cup raisins
¼ cup water

Place wholemeal flour, flour, cocoa, baking powder and butter in a food processor, and blend until mix resembles fine breadcrumbs. Add all the remaining ingredients and blend until combined. Transfer cake mixture into prepared (base lined with greaseproof paper and greased) ring tin, and spread out evenly. Bake for 35 minutes at 160°C (325°F). Once cool, store in refrigerator.

**Makes 1 cake**

**Divided into 20 equal servings, each serving provides approximately:**
**1½ CARBOHYDRATE CHOICES, ½ PROTEIN CHOICE,**
**13g carbohydrate, 3.5g protein, 3.5g fat, 1.5g dietary fibre, 100 kcal (420 kJ)**

# Spicy Carrot Cake

### Dairy free

A delightfully moist and morish cake.

2 *cups wholemeal flour*
2 *teaspoons baking soda*
1 *teaspoon baking powder*
1 ½ *teaspoons cinnamon*
1 ½ *teaspoons mixed spice*
1 *teaspoon ground ginger*
½ *cup vegetable oil*
3 *eggs*
½ *cup water*
1 *tablespoon liquid artificial sweetener (equivalent to ½ cup sugar)*
4 *cups grated carrot, lightly packed (360g)*

Mix dry ingredients together in a small bowl. In a large bowl whip oil, eggs, water and sweetener together well until thick and frothy. Fold dry ingredients gently through this egg mixture. Finally, add grated carrot and mix carefully to combine. Transfer cake mixture into a prepared (base lined with greaseproof paper and greased) 20 x 20cm cake tin. Bake at 160°C (325°F) for 50-60 minutes, or until cooked. Once cool, store in refrigerator.

*Makes 1 cake*

**Divided into 20 equal servings, each serving provides approximately:**
**1 CARBOHYDRATE CHOICE, ½ PROTEIN CHOICE, 1 FAT &**
**OIL CHOICE,**
**11g carbohydrate, 3g protein, 7g fat, 2g dietary fibre, 120 kcal**
**(480 kJ)**

# Orange Peanut Cake

## Dairy free

A moist, nutty cake which is very quick to prepare. It is not particularly sweet — you may prefer to add a little liquid artificial sweetener.

1 *orange*
1 *cup peanuts*
1 *cup raisins*
⅓ *cup vegetable oil*
2 *tablespoons honey*
2 *eggs*
¾ *cup water*
1 *cup wholemeal flour*
1 *cup flour*
1 *teaspoon baking powder*
1 *teaspoon bicarbonate of soda*

Grate rind off orange (retain), then remove and discard pith. Cut orange in half and remove pips. Place orange halves, peanuts and raisins in a food processor and blend until all large chunks of orange have been pulped down into small pieces. Add grated orange rind with remaining ingredients and blend to combine. Transfer cake mixture into prepared (based lined with greaseproof paper and greased) 20 x 20cm cake tin. Bake for 35-40 minutes at 160°C (325°F). Once cool, store in refrigerator.

*Makes 1 cake*

**Divided into 20 equal servings, each serving provides approximately:
2 CARBOHYDRATE CHOICES, ½ PROTEIN CHOICE, 1 FAT &
OIL CHOICE,
18g carbohydrate, 4.5g protein, 8.5g fat, 2.5g dietary fibre, 160 kcal
(680 kJ)**

# Celebration Cake

A rich fruit cake to grace any special occasion.

450g currants
300g sultanas
1½ cups grated carrot, lightly packed (135g)
⅓ cup whisky
1⅓ cups unsweetened apple juice
100g dried apricots, chopped
100g butter
2 teaspoons bicarbonate of soda
2½ cups wholemeal flour
2 teaspoons baking powder
1½ teaspoons cinnamon
2 eggs

Place currants, sultanas, grated carrot and whisky in a large mixing bowl. Heat apple juice, chopped apricots and butter together in a large pot until butter melted. Dissolve bicarbonate of soda in this hot mixture, then pour this over fruit. Add dry ingredients and eggs and mix well. Transfer mixture to a prepared (based lined with greaseproof paper and greased) 23 x 23cm cake tin. Decorate surface with a few whole or chopped walnuts if desired (see cake decorating ideas p. 125). Bake at 160ºC (325ºF) until cooked, approximately 55 minutes.

---

*Makes 1 large cake*

**Divided into 64 equal servings, each serving provides approximately:**
**1½ CARBOHYDRATE CHOICES, ½ FAT & OIL CHOICE,**
**13g carbohydrate, 1g protein, 1.5g fat, 2g dietary fibre, 71 kcal (300 kJ)**

**HIGH-FRUIT RECIPE**

*Note: To make it easier to cut into serving-sized portions, cut cake into quarters first, then each quarter into 16 servings.*

---

# Pineapple Fruit Cake

**Dairy free if dairy-free margarine used instead of butter**

A moist fruit cake with a surprisingly rich flavour when you consider the ingredients used — no essences, alcohol, peel or nuts are included.

*230g can crushed pineapple in unsweetened pineapple juice, undrained*
*1 cup each raisins, sultanas and currants*
*75g butter*
*1 teaspoon mixed spice*
*1 cup water*
*1½ teaspoons bicarbonate of soda*
*2 cups wholemeal flour*
*1½ teaspoons baking powder*
*2 eggs*

Place undrained pineapple, dried fruit, butter, mixed spice and water in a large pot. Heat gently until butter melts, then bring to the boil and simmer for 3 minutes. Remove from heat, add bicarbonate of soda and mix in. Cover and leave to cool until at least tepid (if you add remaining ingredients while the fruit mixture is still hot, they start to cook in the bowl). Add wholemeal flour, baking powder and eggs to cooled fruit mixture and mix thoroughly. Transfer cake mixture to prepared (base lined with greaseproof paper and greased) 20 x 20cm cake tin. Bake at 160°C (325°F) for 1 hour, or until cooked. Check after 45 minutes — if top well browned, cover with tinfoil for remainder of baking to avoid surface burning. For best flavour, keep for 1-2 days before eating.

*Makes 1 cake*
**Divided into 25 equal servings, each serving provides approximately:**
**2 CARBOHYDRATE CHOICES, ½ FAT & OIL CHOICE,**
**21g carbohydrate, 2.5g protein, 3g fat, 2.5g dietary fibre, 120 kcal (490 kJ)**
**HIGH-FRUIT RECIPE**

# FROZEN DELIGHTS

This section contains recipes for light and refreshing frozen desserts. These are best made on the day required, or one day ahead of time. If frozen for more than a day or two, these desserts tend to go very icy and hard.

If this does happen to you, do not despair — simply remove the frozen dessert from the freezer about 15 minutes before you intend serving it. This allows for partial thawing to occur, which makes for much easier handling.

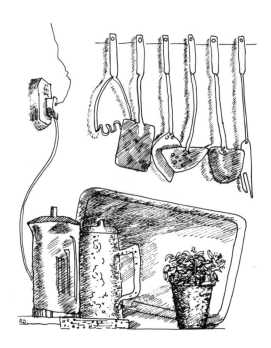

# Boysenberry Crush

A scrumptious summer dessert — serve on its own garnished with mint or angelica. When the weather is cooler, use chocolate sauce (see recipe p. 101) or chocolate custard (see recipe p. 100), to take the chill off this dessert.

2 teaspoons gelatine
¼ cup water
250g boysenberries, washed and drained
1 cup unsweetened low-fat natural yoghurt
juice of 1 orange made up to ¼ cup with water
1 tablespoon liquid artificial sweetener (equivalent to ½ cup sugar)
2 egg whites

Sprinkle gelatine over water in a small saucepan, then set aside to allow the gelatine to hydrate. Place boysenberries in a blender and blend to a pulp. Heat gelatine and water while stirring until gelatine is dissolved. Add to boysenberry pulp along with the yoghurt, orange juice and sweetener. Blend to mix. Pour into an ice-cream tray and freeze until ice crystals form a 1cm thick layer around the sides of the tray. Remove from freezer and beat thoroughly. Beat egg whites until stiff and fold through berry mixture. Freeze in ice-cream tray(s) until firm.

**Makes 8 servings**

**Each serving provides approximately:**
**½ CARBOHYDRATE CHOICE, ½ PROTEIN CHOICE,**
**4.5g carbohydrate, 3g protein, 0.6g fat, 1.5g dietary fibre, 37 kcal (150 kJ)**

**HIGH-FRUIT RECIPE**

# Minted Sorbet

An exquisitely cool dessert — use to refresh your palate at the end of a hot summer's day. Serve on its own, or as an accompaniment to fresh strawberries.

1 *cup chopped mint leaves, firmly packed*
½ *cup boiling water*
1 *teaspoon gelatine*
¼ *cup water*
2 *eggs, separated*
1 *tablespoon lemon juice*
1 *tablespoon liquid artificial sweetener (equivalent to ½ cup sugar)*
250ml (1 cup) *low-fat cream*

Pour boiling water over chopped mint leaves, cover and leave to stand for 20 minutes, then strain (retain liquid). Sprinkle gelatine over surface of ¼ cup water in a small saucepan, leave to hydrate for 5 minutes, then heat while stirring until gelatine dissolved. Beat egg yolks, lemon juice, sweetener, cream, mint extract and dissolved gelatine together, then transfer to a freezing tray (or other suitable shallow container) and freeze until ice crystals start to form around the edges. Beat again, then carefully fold through stiffly beaten egg whites. Return to freezing tray and freeze until firm. Serve garnished with mint.

**Makes 8 servings**

**Each serving provides approximately:**
**½ PROTEIN CHOICE, ½ FAT & OIL CHOICE,**
**1.5g carbohydrate, 3g protein, 5g fat, 66 kcal (280 kJ)**

# Strawberry Water Ice

**Dairy free**

This is a delicious refreshing way to round off a special summer meal.

3 *cups (375g) strawberries*
1 *cup water*
6 *sachets aspartame sweetener (equivalent to ¼ cup sugar)*
2 *tablespoons lemon juice*
2 *tablespoons Grand Marnier or Cointreau*

Place washed and hulled strawberries together with all the other ingredients in blender. Blend until fruit pulped. Push the strawberry mixture through a fine sieve. Freeze in a shallow container. When ready to serve, run a fork across the surface of the ice so that it flakes and separates. Fork into chilled individual serving glasses (the ice melts more slowly in cold glasses).

*Makes 6 servings*

*Each serving provides approximately:*
½ **CARBOHYDRATE CHOICE,**
**6.5g *carbohydrate*, 0.5g *protein*, 0.3g *fat*, 1g *dietary fibre*, 41 *kcal* (170 *kJ*)**

**HIGH-FRUIT RECIPE**

# Frozen Tropical Sherbet

Serve on its own, with fruit, or with chocolate sauce (see recipe p. 101). Freeze ½ cup quantities in small pottles for after-school treats for children on hot summer days. This recipe does not work well as ice-blocks because the sticks come out too easily.

*Note: Evaporated milk must be well chilled first so that it whips satisfactorily.*

1 ripe banana, mashed
½ cup unsweetened orange juice
230g can crushed pineapple in unsweetened pineapple juice, undrained
2 tablespoons lemon juice
1 cup evaporated milk, well chilled

Combine mashed banana, orange juice, undrained pineapple and lemon juice. Pour into a shallow container and chill. Once fruit mixture is chilled, whip the chilled evaporated milk until it is thick and foamy. Fold fruit mixture gently into this whipped evaporated milk. Return mixture to shallow container and freeze until firm.

**Makes 12 servings**

**Serving size = ½ cup (approximately)**
**1 CARBOHYDRATE CHOICE,**
**7.5g carbohydrate, 2g protein, 1.5g fat, 0.3g dietary fibre, 52 kcal (220 kJ)**

**HIGH-FRUIT RECIPE**

# COOL AND LIGHT DESSERTS

This section contains a variety of chilled desserts, all of which are reasonably light on calories — no more than 120 kcal (510 kJ) per serving.

Many of these recipes are gelatine-based. For best results allow the gelatine to hydrate in a small volume of liquid for about 5 minutes (in other words let the gelatine absorb the liquid) before heating to dissolve it. Make sure that the gelatine does dissolve completely to avoid any gelatinous lumps in the end product.

# Lemon Bliss

A cold lemon souffle which just melts in your mouth.

*Note: Evaporated milk must be chilled thoroughly before this dessert can be prepared.*

1 tablespoon gelatine
¼ cup cold water
3 eggs, separated
grated rind and juice of 2 lemons
1 tablespoon liquid artificial sweetener (equivalent to ½ cup sugar)
½ cup evaporated milk, well chilled

Sprinkle gelatine over water in a small saucepan, then heat while stirring until gelatine dissolves. Set aside to cool. Place egg yolks, lemon rind and juice, and sweetener together in a bowl, then whisk until combined and slightly thickened. In a large bowl beat egg whites until stiff. Carefully fold egg yolk mixture and dissolved gelatine through whipped egg whites. Rinse bowl used for egg yolk mixture, then reuse it to whip evaporated milk until thick. Fold whipped evaporated milk carefully into mixture. Pour mixture into 6 individual serving dishes, or one large serving dish (or a jelly mould if you wish to turn it out onto a flat plate to serve). Refrigerate until set.

**Makes 6 servings**

**Each serving provides approximately:**
**1 PROTEIN CHOICE,**
**2.5g carbohydrate, 6.5g protein, 4.5g fat, 0.3g dietary fibre, 78 kcal (320 kJ)**

# Banana Yoghurt Slice

This slice can be used either as a dessert, or as a slice for morning or afternoon tea.

**Base**
125g wine biscuits, crushed
75g butter, melted

**Topping**
¼ cup water
4 teaspoons gelatine
500g unsweetened low-fat natural yoghurt
2 very ripe bananas, mashed (should yield about ⅔ cup)
1 tablespoon liquid artificial sweetener (equivalent to ½ cup sugar)
juice of 1 lemon

Mix melted butter through crushed wine biscuits. Spread evenly over base of round 25cm serving dish or other dish of similar size. Press firmly into place. Refrigerate while preparing topping.
    Place water in saucepan. Sprinkle gelatine over water, allow to hydrate for 5 minutes, then heat while stirring until gelatine dissolves. Add gelatine mixture to balance of ingredients in food processor and blend until smooth. Pour over base and refrigerate to set.

---

*Makes 16 servings*

*Each serving provides approximately*:
**1 CARBOHYDRATE CHOICE, ½ PROTEIN CHOICE, ½ FAT & OIL CHOICE,**
**10g carbohydrate, 3g protein, 5g fat, 0.4g dietary fibre, 96 kcal (400 kJ)**

---

# Pears in Lemon Jelly

**Dairy free**

1 *tablespoon gelatine*
¼ *cup water*
425g *can pear quarters in unsweetened fruit juice*
*rind of* 1 *lemon*
*juice of* 2 *lemons*
¼ *teaspoon cinnamon*
3 *whole cloves*
¾ *cup water*

Sprinkle gelatine over ¼ cup water in a cup and leave to hydrate. Drain fruit juice off pears (approximately ¾ cup) into a saucepan and add lemon rind and juice, cinnamon, cloves and ¾ cup water. Bring to the boil and simmer for 5 minutes. Remove from heat. Add hydrated gelatine and stir until dissolved. Strain mixture (use a cloth if you want a clear jelly), then pour over pear quarters arranged in a jelly mould, or in 4 individual serving dishes. Refrigerate to set.

*Makes 4 servings*

*Each serving provides approximately:*
1½ **CARBOHYDRATE CHOICES,**
13g *carbohydrate,* 2.5g *protein,* 0.1g *fat,* 0.5g *dietary fibre,* 63 *kcal* (260 *kJ*)

**HIGH-FRUIT RECIPE**

# Berry Yoghurt Jelly

¾ cup unsweetened low-fat natural yoghurt
1 tablespoon gelatine
¾ cup unsweetened orange juice
4 sachets aspartame sweetener (equivalent to 3 tablespoons sugar)
¾ cup strawberries, raspberries or boysenberries (hulled, washed and drained)

Put yoghurt in a bowl, sprinkle gelatine over the yoghurt and leave to stand for 5 minutes. Heat the orange juice to boiling point. Add to the yoghurt and mix until the gelatine is dissolved. Next add sweetener and mix thoroughly. Cover and chill mixture until it has the consistency of unbeaten egg white. Stir the berries through the yoghurt mixture. Pour into 4 individual serving dishes or a jelly mould, and chill until set.

**Makes 4 servings**

**Each serving provides approximately:**
**1 CARBOHYDRATE CHOICE, ½ PROTEIN CHOICE,**
**9.5g carbohydrate, 4.5g protein, 0.8g fat, 0.4g dietary fibre, 63 kcal
(270 kJ)**

**HIGH-FRUIT RECIPE**

# Ambrosia with Oranges

This is a cool citrus delight.

*1¼ cups unsweetened low-fat natural yoghurt*
*½ cup low-fat cream*
*grated rind of 1 lemon*
*1 tablespoon lemon juice*
*grated rind of ½ orange*
*1 tablespoon fine oatmeal*
*3 sachets aspartame sweetener (equivalent to 2 tablespoons sugar)*
*3 oranges*

To make ambrosia simply mix yoghurt, cream, lemon rind and juice, orange rind, oatmeal and sweetener. Prepare orange segments using a serrated knife: firstly peel off the skin and the membrane on the outside of the segments, then remove flesh of segments from between the membrane dividers. Serve in parfait glasses. Place a layer of orange segments in the bottom followed by a layer of ambrosia, then repeat these layers once again. Garnish with mint or orange zest.

**Makes 4 servings**

**Each serving provides approximately:**
**1½ CARBOHYDRATE CHOICES, 1 PROTEIN CHOICE,**
**14g carbohydrate, 5.5g protein, 5g fat, 1.5g dietary fibre, 120 kcal (510 kJ)**

**HIGH-FRUIT RECIPE**

Here are two delectable mousse recipes — made with low-fat cream they have the wonderful creamy consistency generally associated with a mousse dessert, but without such excessive calories.

# Strawberry Mousse

This is an excellent way to utilise strawberries which are just past their best and not really suitable for serving fresh. Frozen strawberries can be used too for an out-of-season treat.

2 *teaspoons gelatine*
*½ cup water*
*300g strawberries, washed and drained*
*250ml (1 cup) low-fat cream (or 250g low-fat sour cream)*
*1 tablespoon lemon juice*
*1 tablespoon liquid artificial sweetener (equivalent to ½ cup sugar)*
*2 egg whites*

Sprinkle gelatine over surface of water in a small saucepan and allow to hydrate for 5 minutes. Place strawberries, cream (or sour cream), lemon juice and sweetener in a blender. Heat gelatine and water while stirring until gelatine is dissolved. Add to other ingredients in blender and blend until the strawberries are broken up and all the ingredients are combined. Beat egg whites until soft peaks form, then fold the strawberry mixture gently through the beaten egg whites until just combined. Pour into 6 individual serving dishes. Refrigerate until set. Serve garnished with fresh mint.

*Makes 6 servings*

*Each serving provides approximately*:
**½ CARBOHYDRATE CHOICE, ½ PROTEIN CHOICE, ½ FAT & OIL CHOICE,**
**5.5g *carbohydrate*, 4g *protein*, 5g *fat*, 0.9g *dietary fibre*, 84 *kcal* (350 *kJ*)**

**HIGH-FRUIT RECIPE**

# Chocolate Mousse

1 *cup* Trim *milk*
2 *teaspoons gelatine*
¼ *cup water*
3 *tablespoons cocoa*
¼ *cup water*
2 *eggs*
250ml (1 *cup*) *low-fat cream*
1 *tablespoon brandy*
1 *tablespoon liquid artificial sweetener* (*equivalent to* ½ *cup sugar*)

First heat milk until almost boiling then set aside to cool slightly. Sprinkle gelatine over surface of ¼ cup water and leave to hydrate. Heat cocoa and second ¼ cup water in a medium-sized saucepan, while stirring, until a smooth cocoa paste is achieved. Separate eggs, retain whites and whisk yolks into cocoa paste. Add milk to this mixture slowly while stirring. Heat over medium heat until this custard starts to thicken — stir constantly and *do not allow to boil* — then remove from heat. Heat gelatine and water, again while stirring, until gelatine dissolved.

Mix dissolved gelatine, low-fat cream, brandy and sweetener into custard. Cover surface with plastic film to prevent skin formation, and refrigerate until it has thickened to the consistency of egg white. Beat the two egg whites retained earlier until soft peaks form. Gently fold custard mixture through these beaten egg whites, then divide mixture evenly into 6 individual serving dishes. Refrigerate until set.

**Makes 6 servings**

**Each serving provides approximately:**
½ **CARBOHYDRATE CHOICE, 1 PROTEIN CHOICE, ½ FAT &
OIL CHOICE,**
**4.5g carbohydrate, 7g protein, 8g fat, 120 kcal (510 kJ)**

# MILK DESSERTS

This section contains a selection of hot and cold milk desserts. The Spanish Cream and Ice-Cream Pudding recipes could have been included under *Cool and Light Desserts*, but they are essentially milk desserts. Most of these recipes, like those in the *Cool and Light Desserts* section, provide no more than 120 kcal (510 kJ) per serving — the Coffee Creams, and Lemon and Sultana Rice Pudding recipes are the two exceptions.

## Creamy Rice Pudding

A simple pudding which can be served hot or cold, on its own, or with fruit.

*⅓ cup short grain rice*
*2 cups Trim milk*
*2 eggs, separated*
*1 teaspoon vanilla essence*
*6 sachets aspartame sweetener (equivalent to ¼ cup sugar)*

Place rice and milk in top of double boiler, cook over boiling water for 45 minutes, then remove from heat. Fold egg yolks and vanilla through cooked rice. Beat egg whites until stiff, then fold rice mixture and sweetener through beaten egg whites and serve.

*Makes 6 servings*

*Each serving provides approximately*:
1½ CARBOHYDRATE CHOICES, 1 PROTEIN CHOICE,
*15g carbohydrate, 6.5g protein, 2.5g fat, 0.3g dietary fibre*, 110 *kcal*
(450 *kJ*)

# Lemon and Sultana Rice Pudding

This is a tasty variation of the preceding recipe. The juice and rind of an orange can be used instead of the lemon if preferred.

⅓ *cup short grain rice*
2 *cups Trim milk*
⅓ *cup sultanas*
½ *teaspoon cinnamon*
2 *eggs, separated*
*juice and rind of 1 lemon*
6 *sachets aspartame sweetener (equivalent to ¼ cup sugar)*

Place rice, milk, sultanas and cinnamon in top of double boiler, cook over boiling water for 45 minutes, then remove from heat. Lightly beat egg yolks, lemon rind and juice together, then fold through cooked rice mixture. Beat egg whites until stiff, then fold rice mixture and sweetener through beaten egg whites. Serve warm, or chill and serve cold.

*Makes 6 servings*

*Each serving provides approximately:*
**2 CARBOHYDRATE CHOICES, 1 PROTEIN CHOICE,**
**21g *carbohydrate*, 6.5g *protein*, 2.5g *fat*, 1g *dietary fibre*, 130 *kcal* (540 *kJ*)**

# Lemon Cheese Pudding

This self-saucing lemon pudding is simple to make and always popular.

*3 tablespoons flour*
*1 tablespoon butter*
*rind and juice of 1 lemon*
*1 cup Trim milk*
*2 teaspoons liquid artificial sweetener (equivalent to ¼ cup sugar)*
*2 eggs, separated*

Place flour and butter in a food processor and blend until butter is rubbed through flour. Add lemon rind and juice, milk, sweetener and egg yolks. Blend to combine. In a bowl, beat egg whites until stiff, then carefully fold in lemon mixture. Pour into a pie dish. Bake for 35-40 minutes at 180ºC (350ºF), with the pie dish sitting in a pan of hot water. Do not overcook or the pudding will be all topping and no sauce.

**Makes 4 servings**

**Each serving provides approximately:**
**1 CARBOHYDRATE CHOICE, 1 PROTEIN CHOICE, ½ FAT & OIL CHOICE,**
**8g carbohydrate, 7g protein, 6.5g fat, 0.6g dietary fibre, 120 kcal (490 kJ)**

# Ice-Cream Pudding

A cool companion for fruit.

1¾ *cups Trim milk*
25g *butter*
3 *tablespoons flour*
1 *egg*
¼ *cup Trim milk, extra*
1 *teaspoon vanilla essence*
6 *sachets aspartame sweetener (equivalent to ¼ cup sugar)*

Heat 1¾ cups milk until almost boiling. In another saucepan, melt butter then stir in flour to make a roux. Add hot milk gradually to this roux, stirring all the time to ensure a smooth mixture. Beat egg and extra ¼ cup milk together and add this to the hot milk mix. Bring mix to the boil and simmer until it thickens, stirring all the time. Remove from heat and allow to cool a little. Mix in vanilla essence and aspartame sweetener. Serve chilled.

**Makes 6 servings**

**Each serving provides approximately:**
**1 CARBOHYDRATE CHOICE, 1 PROTEIN CHOICE,**
**9g carbohydrate, 5g protein, 5g fat, 0.2g dietary fibre, 100 kcal**
**(410 kJ)**

# Coffee Creams

This dessert has a lovely creamy consistency despite no cream being added.

*600ml Trim milk*
*¼ cup strong black coffee*
*4 egg yolks*
*1 tablespoon liquid artificial sweetener (equivalent to ½ cup sugar)*
*2 tablespoons cornflour*
*1 tablespoon brandy*

Using a heavy-bottomed saucepan, heat the milk until it just comes to the boil. Remove from heat, add the coffee and mix. Whisk the egg yolks with the artificial sweetener until combined then pour into hot milk, mixing well. Return to heat, stirring constantly with a wooden spoon until the mixture coats the back of the spoon. Do not boil. Remove from heat but continue stirring for a minute to ensure the mixture does not burn on to the bottom of the pot. Mix the cornflour with the brandy until smooth, then add to the mixture. Stir over low heat until thickened. Remove from heat and pour into 4 individual serving dishes. Leave at room temperature until cool, then transfer to refrigerator. Serve very cold.

**Makes 4 servings**

**Each serving provides approximately:**
**1 CARBOHYDRATE CHOICE, 1½ PROTEIN CHOICES,**
**12g carbohydrate, 9.5g protein, 6.5g fat, 150 kcal (640 kJ)**

# Spanish Cream

This simple dessert makes a lovely light accompaniment to fresh fruit salad or fruit canned or preserved with no added sugar.

1 *tablespoon gelatine*
2½ *cups Trim milk*
2 *eggs, separated*
3 *sachets aspartame sweetener (equivalent to 2 tablespoons sugar)*
1 *teaspoon vanilla essence*

Sprinkle gelatine over the surface of ½ cup milk in a saucepan. Leave this to stand while you lightly beat the egg yolks with another ½ cup milk. Then heat milk and gelatine while stirring until gelatine dissolves, add remaining 1½ cups milk and heat until almost boiling. Add the egg yolk mixture and stir over low heat with a wooden spoon until the mixture coats the back of the spoon (*do not allow to boil*). Cool until tepid, then mix in sweetener and vanilla essence. Finally, fold in stiffly beaten egg whites. Pour into a serving dish and refrigerate until set.

**Makes 6 servings**

**Each serving provides approximately:**
**½ CARBOHYDRATE CHOICE, 1 PROTEIN CHOICE,**
**6g carbohydrate, 8g protein, 2.5g fat, 79 kcal (330 kJ)**

Note: *There are many delicious variations you can make from this recipe, for example omit the vanilla essence and add the juice and rind of a lemon or orange. A word of warning however — do not add orange or lemon juice to hot milk and egg mixture or it will curdle, wait until it is cool.*

# BAKED AND STEAMED PUDDINGS

This type of dessert is generally higher in carbohydrate content than frozen, chilled and milk desserts. To keep the CARBOHYDRATE CHOICES per serving down to a reasonable level the servings have to be kept reasonably small. For this reason allow some leeway with serving numbers if you are feeding predominantly non-diabetics, especially ravenous children or teenagers!

I have purposely tried to select recipes for this section that are reasonably low in fat. This was not very easy as many baked puddings, in particular, are high in fat. All these recipes provide 5g fat or less per serving, the one exception being the apricot sponge pudding at 8.5g fat per serving.

A number of these recipes are made using a rolled-oat pie base (or a variation thereof), which is a very versatile, low-fat, sweet pastry substitute. We find this recipe very useful and hope you do too.

# Rolled Oat Pie Base

## Dairy free

Most pies and tarts are high in fat because of the pastry. This versatile low-fat substitute for sweet pastry allows you to make a variety of low fat pies. It can be used either as an uncooked base, (refrigerate to firm), a crisp crust (bake blind filled with uncooked beans or rice for about 10 minutes at 180ºC [350ºF]) or as a crust for cooked pies.

1¼ *cups rolled oats*
½ *cup wheatgerm*
⅓ *cup sultanas*
2 *teaspoons honey*
¼ *cup water*
½ *teaspoon cinnamon (optional)*

Combine all ingredients in a food processor until they begin to stick together. Spread mixture evenly over base and up sides of greased pie dish. Press down firmly.

*Makes sufficient to line base and sides of a round 23cm pie dish.*

*1 serving = ⅛ recipe*
1½ **CARBOHYDRATE CHOICES**, ½ **PROTEIN CHOICE**,
*16g carbohydrate, 3g protein, 1g fat, 1.5g dietary fibre, 85 kcal (360 kJ)*

# Pumpkin Pie

A winter favourite. I have included a little salt, adjust quantity according to your own palate.

**Base**
*Rolled oat pie base (see recipe p. 92)*

**Filling**
1 *cup cooked pumpkin pulp*
½ *cup Trim milk*
1 *egg, beaten*
1 *tablespoon flour*
½ *teaspoon cinnamon*
¼ *teaspoon ginger*
*pinch nutmeg*
2 *teaspoons brown sugar*
1 *teaspoon liquid artificial sweetener (equivalent to 2 tablespoons sugar)*
¼ *teaspoon salt (optional)*

Press rolled oat base down firmly over base and sides of greased, round 23cm pie dish.

To prepare pumpkin pulp, simmer peeled pumpkin until soft, drain well, then mash. Mix all ingredients together and pour into base. Bake at 180°C (350°F) until pumpkin filling cooked through (check by inserting tip of knife into centre), approximately 30 minutes.

*Makes 1 pie*

**Divided into 8 equal servings, each serving provides approximately:
2 CARBOHYDRATE CHOICES, ½ PROTEIN CHOICE,
20g carbohydrate, 4.5g protein, 2g fat, 2g dietary fibre, 120 kcal
(480 kJ)**

# Blueberry Tart

**Dairy free**

A touch of allspice enhances the flavour of this delicious tart.

## Base
Rolled oat pie base (see recipe p. 92) made using ¼ teaspoon ground allspice instead of cinnamon.

## Filling
2 tablespoons lemon juice
2 tablespoons cold water
1 tablespoon liquid artificial sweetener (equivalent to ½ cup sugar)
2 tablespoons arrowroot (or cornflour)
¼ teaspoon ground allspice
450g blueberries (fresh, or thawed frozen berries)

Press rolled oat base down firmly over base and sides of greased, round 23cm pie dish.

Place lemon juice, cold water, sweetener, arrowroot (or cornflour) and allspice in a small saucepan. Mix to a smooth paste. Heat over medium heat, while stirring, until thickened. Stir paste through blueberries, then spread this blueberry filling evenly over base. Bake for 15-20 minutes at 180°C (350°F) to crisp base and heat the filling thoroughly. Serve hot with a little ice-cream or whipped cream.

*Makes 1 pie*

**Divided into 8 equal servings, each serving provides approximately:
2½ CARBOHYDRATE CHOICES, ½ PROTEIN CHOICE,
26g carbohydrate, 3.5g protein, 1.5g fat, 2.5g dietary fibre, 120 kcal
(520 kJ)**

# Orange Custard Pie

The carob-flavoured base of this low-fat pie delightfully comple-
ments the orange custard filling.

*Note: Before juicing orange to make base, grate off the rind and retain for use
in filling.*

## Base
1 ¼ *cups rolled oats*
½ *cup wheatgerm*
⅓ *cup sultanas*
*juice of 1 orange made up to* ¼ *cup with water*
2 *tablespoons carob powder*

## Filling
3 *tablespoons flour*
1 *tablespoon butter*
1 *tablespoon honey*
*rind of 2 oranges*
*juice of 1 orange*
1 *cup Trim milk*
2 *eggs, separated*

Combine all base ingredients in a food processor until they begin
to stick together. Press mix firmly over base and sides of greased,
round 23cm pie dish.

Place flour and butter in a food processor and blend until butter
is rubbed through flour. Add honey, orange rind and juice, milk
and egg yolks. Blend to combine. In a bowl beat egg whites until
stiff, then carefully fold in the orange mixture. Pour custard filling
over base. Bake at 180°C (350°F) until custard filling cooked through
(check by inserting tip of knife in centre), approximately 30 minutes.

*Makes 1 pie*

**Divided into 8 equal servings, each serving provides approximately:**
**2½ CARBOHYDRATE CHOICES, 1 PROTEIN CHOICE,**
**24g carbohydrate, 6.5g protein, 4.5g fat, 2g dietary fibre, 150 kcal**
**(650 kJ)**

# Apricot Sponge Pudding

**Dairy free**

This quick to prepare pudding can be made with fruits other than apricots too, just use 1½-2 cups of whatever unsweetened (or artificially sweetened) stewed, bottled or canned fruit you have available. Serve warm with custard (see recipe p. 99), or a little whipped cream.

410g can apricots in unsweetened fruit juice
2 eggs
2 tablespoons vegetable oil
2 tablespoons water
2 teaspoons liquid artificial sweetener (equivalent to ¼ cup sugar)
¾ cup flour
¼ cup coconut
2 teaspoons baking powder

Place apricots (or other fruit you have selected) in an ovenproof dish. If there is a lot of liquid around the fruit, drain some away. Heat fruit in oven while you prepare the batter for the sponge topping. Beat eggs, oil, water and sweetener together until thick and frothy. Add flour, coconut and baking powder, and mix to combine. Pour over the top of the hot fruit. Bake for 30-40 minutes at 180ºC (350ºF).

*Makes 6 servings*

*Each serving provides approximately:*
**2 CARBOHYDRATE CHOICES, 1 PROTEIN CHOICE, ½ FAT & OIL CHOICE,**
**22g carbohydrate, 5g protein, 8.5g fat, 2g dietary fibre, 180 kcal (760 kJ)**

# Chocolate Steamed Pudding

A family favourite. Serve with chocolate custard (see recipe p. 100) or chocolate sauce (see recipe p. 101).

¾ *cup wholemeal flour*
½ *cup flour*
2 *tablespoons cocoa*
1 *teaspoon bicarbonate of soda*
1 *teaspoon baking powder*
25g *butter* ·
1 *egg*
1½ *teaspoons liquid artificial sweetener (equivalent to 3 tablespoons sugar)*
½ *cup unsweetened low-fat natural yoghurt*
⅓ *cup water*

Put dry ingredients and butter in a food processor and blend until mix resembles fine breadcrumbs. Add all the rest of the ingredients and blend until combined. Transfer pudding mixture into a greased steam pudding bowl with 750ml (3 cup) capacity. Cover and steam for 1 hour.

---

*Makes 1 steam pudding*

*Divided into 8 equal servings, each serving provides approximately:*
1½ **CARBOHYDRATE CHOICES,** ½ **PROTEIN CHOICE,** ½ **FAT & OIL CHOICE,**
*17g carbohydrate, 4.5g protein, 4.5g fat, 2g dietary fibre, 120 kcal (520 kJ)*

---

# Sago Plum Pudding

A different steamed pudding. Serve with custard (see recipe p. 99), lemon sauce (see recipe p. 102), or for a real festival of flavours, orange brandy custard (see recipe p. 137).

¼ cup sago
1 cup Trim milk
1 teaspoon bicarbonate of soda
1½ cups (90g) soft wholegrain breadcrumbs
½ cup sultanas
¼ cup chopped dates
1 tablespoon liquid artificial sweetener (equivalent to ½ cup sugar)
25g butter, melted
2 eggs

Wash sago in a fine strainer under cold running water, then soak in milk overnight (or at least 4 hours). Stir crushed bicarbonate of soda into milk and sago mixture. Add remaining ingredients and mix well. Transfer the pudding mixture to a greased pudding bowl of at least 1 litre (4 cup) capacity. Cover and steam for 3 hours.

**Makes 1 steam pudding**

**Divided into 8 equal servings, each serving provides approximately:**
**2 CARBOHYDRATE CHOICES, ½ PROTEIN CHOICE, ½ FAT & OIL CHOICE,**
**21g carbohydrate, 4g protein, 4.5g fat, 1.5g dietary fibre, 140 kcal (590 kJ)**

**HIGH-FRUIT RECIPE**

# CUSTARDS AND SAUCES

A small collection of basic recipes that all provide approximately ½ CARBOHYDRATE CHOICE per serving. This is where the similarities end, however. The Lemon Sauce and Spicy Orange Sauce recipes are low in protein and fat, the milk custards are higher in protein but still reasonably low in fat, but, the chocolate sauce is high in fat and should be used infrequently.

For the fruit sauces a choice of arrowroot or cornflour as thickening agent is given. Using arrowroot produces a more transparent, glossy sauce.

## Vanilla Custard

So versatile and always popular. Serve hot or cold with your favourite fruit, or hot with steamed and baked desserts.

1 *cup Trim milk*
1 *egg*
1 *teaspoon vanilla essence*
3 *sachets aspartame sweetener (equivalent to 2 tablespoons sugar)*

Heat the milk to almost boiling, then allow to cool slightly. Whisk in the egg and heat over low heat (or use a double boiler), stirring constantly, until the custard thickens — *do not boil*. Remove from heat, allow to cool a little, then mix in vanilla essence and aspartame sweetener. If you are going to serve this custard cold, cover the surface with plastic film to avoid skin formation.

*Makes 4 servings, approximately 1 cup*

1 *serving* = ¼ *cup*
½ CARBOHYDRATE CHOICE, ½ PROTEIN CHOICE,
*4g carbohydrate, 4.5g protein, 1.5g fat, 50 kcal (210 kJ)*

# Chocolate Custard

This can also be served hot or cold, as an accompaniment to all sorts of frozen and baked desserts as well as fruit.

1 *cup Trim milk*
1 *tablespoon cocoa*
2 *tablespoons cold water*
1 *egg*
½ *teaspoon vanilla essence*
3 *sachets aspartame sweetener (equivalent to 2 tablespoons sugar)*

First heat milk to almost boiling and leave to cool slightly. In the top section of a double boiler (unheated), mix cocoa and water to a smooth paste. Add egg and whisk to combine. Add milk to this mixture slowly while stirring. Heat, using double boiler, until mixture starts to thicken. Remove from heat. When cooled slightly, add vanilla essence and aspartame sweetener and mix in. If you wish to serve this custard cold, cover the surface with plastic film to avoid a skin forming.

*Makes 4 servings, approximately 1⅓ cups custard*

1 *serving* = ⅓ *cup*
½ **CARBOHYDRATE CHOICE**, ½ **PROTEIN CHOICE**,
**4.5g *carbohydrate*, 4.5g *protein*, 2g *fat*, 54 *kcal* (230 *kJ*)**

# Chocolate Sauce

Serve warm over chocolate steamed pudding, frozen desserts like boysenberry crush (see recipe p. 73), or ice-cream. This recipe will keep up to 10 days in the refrigerator and is very handy to have on stand-by.

*25g butter*
*¼ cup cocoa*
*¾ cup evaporated milk*
*6 sachets aspartame sweetener (equivalent to ¼ cup sugar)*

Melt butter in a small saucepan. Remove from heat, add cocoa and mix until a smooth paste is achieved. Add evaporated milk and heat while stirring constantly until mixture comes to the boil. Reduce heat and simmer, still stirring constantly, until cocoa specks combine with the milk to give a uniformly coloured, smooth sauce. Remove from heat. When cooled to tepid add sweetener and mix through. If you are not going to serve the sauce straight away cover the surface with plastic film to prevent skin formation. There is no need to do this when you store it in the fridge as the skin formed recombines with the sauce on re-heating — remember not to overheat as this could break down the aspartame sweetener and make it lose sweetness.

---

**Makes 8 servings, approximately 1 cup**

**1 serving = 2 tablespoons**
**1 FAT & OIL CHOICE,**
**3.5g carbohydrate, 2.5g protein, 5g fat, 70 kcal (290 kJ)**

---

# Lemon Sauce

This sauce is light and refreshing and quick to make. Serve warm over steamed pudding or frozen dessert.

*rind and juice 1 lemon*
*1 cup water*
*2 tablespoons arrowroot (or cornflour)*
*2 tablespoons water*
*3 sachets aspartame sweetener (equivalent to 2 tablespoons sugar)*

Place rind and juice of lemon, and cup of water, into a small saucepan and bring to the boil. Simmer gently for 5 minutes then add the arrowroot premixed to a smooth paste with the 2 tablespoons water. Stir constantly over medium heat until sauce is thick and smooth. Remove from heat and allow to cool a little (for example while you eat your main course). Add aspartame sweetener, mix to combine and serve.

*Makes 4 servings, approximately 1 cup*

*1 serving = ¼ cup*
**½ CARBOHYDRATE CHOICE,**
**4.5g carbohydrate, 0.1g protein, 0.2g dietary fibre, 18 kcal (76 kJ)**

# Spicy Orange Sauce

### Dairy free

This is another light sauce that is quick to prepare. Use to add extra tang to a steamed fruit pudding, or to take the chill off a frozen dessert.

1 *cup water*
*rind and juice of* 1 *orange*
1 *tablespoon arrowroot (or cornflour)*
½ *teaspoon cinnamon*
6 *sachets aspartame sweetener (equivalent to* ¼ *cup sugar)*

Place water and orange rind in a saucepan. Mix the orange juice, arrowroot (or cornflour) and cinnamon together to form a smooth paste. Add to ingredients in saucepan. Heat while stirring until mixture boils, then simmer gently for 3 minutes. Remove from heat and allow to cool a little. Add aspartame sweetener and mix to combine. Serve warm.

*Makes 4 servings, approximately 1 cup*

1 *serving =* ¼ *cup*
½ **CARBOHYDRATE CHOICE,**
*5g carbohydrate, 0.1g protein, 0.3g dietary fibre, 19 kcal (81 kJ)*

# INDULGENCES
# (RICH DESSERTS)

Perhaps this section would be more aptly entitled surreptitious pleasures. These recipes are high in fat, 6.5-13g fat being provided by individual servings. Needless to say they are high in energy too! Please reserve the use of these recipes for special occasions only. A little indulgence every now and then is acceptable, but only if it is every now and then — not a common occurrence.

I make the same comment as for the *Baked and Steamed Puddings* section with respect to serving sizes. The serving sizes are on the small side to keep the fat and calories per serving down. So, if entertaining a predominantly non-diabetic group, do not expect these desserts to serve quite the number of people indicated by the number of servings stated.

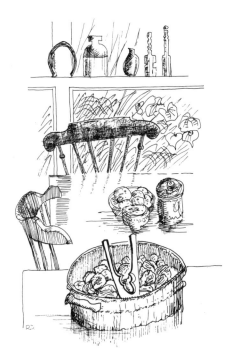

# Fresh Apricot Cheesecake

A scrumptious dessert that will delight your most discerning guests.

**Base**
125g wine biscuits, crushed
⅓ cup coconut, toasted
75g butter, melted

**Topping**
1½ tablespoons gelatine
3 tablespoons cold water
8 fresh apricots
300g low-fat soft cheese
250g low-fat cottage cheese
150ml low-sugar apricot yoghurt
1 teaspoon vanilla essence
1 tablespoon liquid artificial sweetener (equivalent to ½ cup sugar)

Combine all base ingredients. Spread evenly over base of round 25cm serving dish. Press firmly into place. Refrigerate while preparing topping.

Soften gelatine in cold water for 5 minutes. Halve and stone apricots. Set aside 4 halves for decoration and place rest in a blender. Blend until smooth. Heat gelatine and water until gelatine dissolves, add to apricot pulp in blender together with the low-fat soft cheese. Blend until smooth. Add balance of ingredients, and again blend until smooth. Spoon over base in serving dish. Refrigerate to set. Decorate with 4 remaining apricot halves just before serving.

*Makes 1 large cheesecake*

*Divided into 16 equal servings, each serving provides approximately:*
1½ CARBOHYDRATE CHOICES, 1 PROTEIN CHOICE, ½ FAT & OIL CHOICE,
*14g carbohydrate, 6.5g protein, 7.5g fat, 1g dietary fibre, 150 kcal (620 kJ)*

# Apricot and Pineapple Shortcake

**Dairy free if dairy-free margarine used instead of butter**

This shortcake recipe served warm with custard, or a little whipped cream, makes a lovely dessert. It can also be served cold for morning or afternoon tea.

## Shortcake

¾ *cup flour*
½ *cup cornflour*
1 *teaspoon baking powder*
75g *butter*
1 *egg*
1 *teaspoon liquid artificial sweetener (equivalent to 2 tablespoons sugar)*

## Filling

1 *cup apricot and pineapple spread (see recipe p. 32)*

Place flour, cornflour, baking powder and butter in a food processor. Blend until butter rubbed through dry ingredients. Add egg and sweetener and blend until dough formed. Cover dough with plastic wrap and refrigerate for about 45 minutes. Divide dough in half. Roll first half out and use to line base and sides of 20 x 20cm tin or 22cm round dish. Spread cold filling evenly over shortcake base. Roll second half of shortcake dough large enough to cover surface of dish. Before putting top layer of shortcake in place, brush edges of base layer very lightly with water. Position top layer, trim off any excess dough, then pinch edges of surface and base layers of shortcake together. Prick surface layer in several places with a fork. Bake for 30-35 minutes at 180°C (350°F).

---

*Makes 1 pie*

***Divided into 8 equal servings, each serving provides approximately:***
**2½ CARBOHYDRATE CHOICES, ½ PROTEIN CHOICE, 1½ FAT & OIL CHOICES,**

**23g carbohydrate, 3g protein, 9g fat, 2.5g dietary fibre, 180 kcal (750 kJ)**

Note: To use as a cold slice, divide into 12 servings. Each serving provides approximately:
**1½ CARBOHYDRATE CHOICES, 1 FAT & OIL CHOICE,**
**15g carbohydrate, 2g protein, 6g fat, 1.5g dietary fibre, 120 kcal (500 kJ)**

**VARIATIONS:**
**Date and Orange Shortcake**
Use date and orange spread (see recipe p. 33) as filling.
**Apple Shortcake**
Fill with apple pulp, either unsweetened or artificially sweetened to taste.

# Apple Prune Pie

**Dairy free if dairy-free margarine used instead of butter**

A ritzy dessert!

## Pastry
¾ *cup flour*
¼ *cup cornflour*
1 *teaspoon baking powder*
50g *butter*
1 *egg*
1 *teaspoon liquid artificial sweetener (equivalent to 2 tablespoons sugar)*

## Filling
8 *stoned prunes*
⅓ *cup water*
570g *can unsweetened apple slices (or 2 cups unsweetened apple pulp)*
*rind and juice of 1 orange*
¼ *teaspoon cinnamon*
2 *tablespoons flour*

## Topping
⅓ *cup chopped walnuts*
1 *tablespoon brown sugar*
1 *tablespoon butter, melted*

To make pastry, place flour, cornflour, baking powder and butter in blender and blend until mix resembles fine breadcrumbs. Add egg and sweetener and blend until dough formed. Wrap dough in plastic film and refrigerate for 45 minutes, or at least while you prepare filling. Roll pastry out and use to line the base of a round 23cm pie dish. Pinch edges with fingers to produce scalloped effect.

To make filling, place prunes and water in a small saucepan. Bring to the boil and simmer gently, covered, until prunes are soft. Place prunes and cooking liquid in blender, and blend until reasonably smooth. Add the rest of the ingredients and blend to mix. Spread evenly over pastry base.

To make topping, mix the three ingredients together and

sprinkle evenly over the surface of the pie. Bake pie for 1 hour at 180°C (350°F).

---

**Makes 1 large pie**

**Divided into 12 equal servings, each serving provides approximately:**
**2 CARBOHYDRATE CHOICES, 1½ FAT & OIL CHOICES,**
**19g carbohydrate, 2.5g protein, 6.5g fat, 3g dietary fibre, 140 kcal**
**(590 kJ)**

---

# Apple Cream Pie

This appetising pie can be served hot or cold as a dessert, or as a cold slice for morning or afternoon tea.

**Pastry**
¾ cup flour
½ cup cornflour
1 teaspoon baking powder
½ teaspoon cinnamon
grated rind of 1 lemon
75g butter
1 egg yolk
2 tablespoons dry sherry
1 teaspoon liquid artificial sweetener (equivalent to 2 tablespoons sugar)

**Filling**
2 green apples
¼ cup raisins
2 eggs
1 egg white
2 tablespoons flour
grated rind of 1 lemon
⅓ cup Trim milk
250g low-fat sour cream
2 teaspoons liquid artificial sweetener (equivalent to ¼ cup sugar)

Place dry ingredients, lemon rind and butter in blender and blend until mixture resembles fine breadcrumbs. Beat egg yolk, sherry and sweetener together. Add to flour mixture and blend until dough formed. Wrap dough in plastic film and refrigerate for approximately 45 minutes. Roll pastry out and use to line a round 23cm pie dish. Pinch edges with fingers to produce a scalloped effect.

To make filling, peel and core apples, cut into quarters, then slice very thinly. Arrange in overlapping circles in pastry shell. Sprinkle raisins over the top. Blend together eggs, egg white, flour, lemon rind, milk, low-fat sour cream and sweetener. Pour over apples. Bake at 180ºC (350ºF) until cooked, approximately 40-45 minutes.

Makes 1 *large pie*

Divided into 12 *equal servings, each serving provides approximately:*
2 CARBOHYDRATE CHOICES, ½ PROTEIN CHOICE, 1½ FAT &
OIL CHOICES,
19g *carbohydrate, 4.5g protein, 9.5g fat, 1.5g dietary fibre, 180 kcal*
(760 *kJ*)

# Ice-Cream

Making your own ice-cream can be great fun. The number of delicious variations possible is endless — I am sure you can add to my short list here. An ice-cream cake makes a refreshing change from baked cakes for birthdays or other special occasions. Three half recipes of different variations, for example, chocolate, berry and vanilla, layered one on top of each other in a 5 cup (1.25 litre) capacity mould, makes a very impressive cake when removed from the mould and titivated with a little extra whipped cream.

1 teaspoon gelatine
¼ cup water
1 cup Trim milk
1 tablespoon liquid artificial sweetener (equivalent to ½ cup sugar)
2 teaspoons vanilla essence
1 cup cream, whipped

Sprinkle gelatine over surface of water in a medium-sized saucepan and leave to hydrate for 5 minutes. Then heat, while stirring, until gelatine dissolves. Remove from heat and add milk, sweetener and vanilla essence. Mix to combine, then transfer into a freezing tray (or other suitable shallow container). Freeze until ice crystals start to form around the edges. Beat partially frozen mixture with a rotary beater until smooth, then gently fold through the whipped cream. Return to freezing tray and freeze until mushy. Once again beat mixture until smooth, and return to freezing tray as quickly as possible to minimise melting. Freeze until firm, then ice-cream is ready to serve.

---

**Makes 8 servings**

**Each serving provides approximately:**
**2½ FAT & OIL CHOICES,**
**2.5g carbohydrate, 2.5g protein, 12g fat, 130 kcal (550 kJ)**

## VARIATIONS:
### Chocolate Ice-Cream
Heat ¼ cup cocoa and ¼ cup water, while stirring, until a smooth cocoa paste is achieved. Mix this into milk, with vanilla essence and sweetener, before first freezing step.

### Berry Ice-Cream
Fold ½ cup chilled unsweetened berry pulp into ice-cream just before final freezing step. Depending on berries used it may be necessary to add some extra sweetener.

### Apricot Brandy Ice-Cream
Fold into the ice-cream mixture just before the final freezing step, 1 tablespoon brandy and ½ cup chilled unsweetened apricot pulp prepared from cooked or canned fruit that has been well drained. Check sweetness of mixture and add more sweetener if necessary.

### Coffee Walnut Ice-Cream
Add 1 tablespoon instant coffee to milk mixture before first freezing step, and mix in ⅓ cup finely chopped walnuts just before the final freezing step. Check if sweetness is to your liking and add more sweetener if desired.

---

# Cassata

This luscious dessert takes some time to prepare, but the results are worth it. Try it as a deliciously cool alternative to a hot traditional Christmas pudding; it is much more suited to our warm Christmas weather.

It can be made a day or two in advance, but do not try and make it too far ahead of time as, like other homemade ice-cream desserts, it can go hard and icy if left too long.

## Rum Fruit Centre

2 *tablespoons each raisins, sultanas and currants*
2 *dried apricots, finely chopped*
2 *tablespoons rum*
½ *cup cream*
3 *sachets aspartame sweetener (equivalent to 2 tablespoons sugar)*

## Chocolate Peppermint Ice-Cream Exterior

1 *teaspoon gelatine*
¼ *cup water*
¼ *cup cocoa*
¼ *cup water*
1 *cup Trim milk*
2 *teaspoons vanilla essence*
1 *tablespoon liquid artificial sweetener (equivalent to ½ cup sugar)*
4 *small hard peppermints, crushed or finely chopped*
1 *cup cream, whipped*

To make rum fruit centre, pour rum over prepared dried fruit, cover and leave to soak while you prepare chocolate peppermint ice-cream. When you are ready to put this centre into the mould, whip cream and sweetener until stiff. Fold rum-soaked fruit through whipped cream and transfer mixture into mould.

To make chocolate peppermint ice-cream, sprinkle gelatine over ¼ cup water in a small saucepan and leave to hydrate for 5 minutes. Heat cocoa with the other ¼ cup water, while stirring, until a smooth paste is obtained. Heat water and gelatine, again while stirring, until gelatine is dissolved. Mix cocoa paste, dissolved gelatine, milk, vanilla essence, sweetener and crushed peppermints. Freeze this mixture until ice crystals start to form around the edges.

Beat partially frozen mix thoroughly, then fold through whipped cream. Freeze again until mushy. Chill mould for cassata during this freezing step (a mould of approximately 5 cup [1.25 litre] capacity is required). Use ⅔ of ice-cream to line base and sides of mould (if ice-cream is too slushy to handle easily, freeze for a short time to firm it up a little). Fill central cavity with rum fruit centre, then cover with balance of ice-cream. Cover and freeze. To serve, remove from mould. Decorate with a little extra whipped cream and chopped nuts if desired.

---

**Makes 12 servings**

*Each serving provides approximately:*
½ CARBOHYDRATE CHOICE, 2½ FAT & OIL CHOICES,
*6g carbohydrate, 2g protein, 13g fat, 0.5g dietary fibre, 150 kcal (640 kJ)*
HIGH-FRUIT RECIPE

---

# Citrus Supreme Cheesecake

A delicious cheesecake prepared using fresh oranges and lemon.

**Base**
125g wine biscuits, crushed
⅓ cup coconut, toasted
75g butter, melted

**Topping**
1½ tablespoons gelatine
3 tablespoons cold water
2 oranges
1 small lemon
300g low-fat soft cheese
250g low-fat cottage cheese
150ml unsweetened low-fat natural yoghurt
1 tablespoon liquid artificial sweetener (equivalent to ½ cup sugar)

Combine all base ingredients. Spread evenly over base of serving dish (25cm round dish). Press firmly into place. Refrigerate while preparing topping.

Soften gelatine in cold water for 5 minutes. Grate rind from both oranges and the lemon. Squeeze the juice from oranges and lemon. Retain both the juice and the pulp from squeezer (remove pips). Heat gelatine and water until gelatine dissolves and place in blender with low-fat soft cheese. Blend until smooth. Add orange and lemon rind, juice and pulp, then all the remaining ingredients. Again, blend until smooth. Spoon over base in serving dish and refrigerate to set.

*Makes 1 large cheesecake*

**Divided into 16 equal servings, each serving provides approximately:**
**1 CARBOHYDRATE CHOICE, 1 PROTEIN CHOICE, ½ FAT &**
**OIL CHOICE,**
**11g carbohydrate, 6.5g protein, 7.5g fat, 0.8g dietary fibre, 130 kcal**
**(560 kJ)**

# CHILDREN'S PARTY IDEAS

Special occasions like children's birthday parties often create extra headaches for people catering for a diabetic amongst the crowd — whether he or she is the central character or just sharing in the celebrations. I hope some of the ideas provided here may offer a little pain relief for the caterer.

Most normal savoury party dishes: cheerios, potato chips, plain popcorn, pizza, quiches, mouse-traps, hedgehogs (cheese and unsweetened pineapple chunks on toothpicks stuck into half an orange or apple), cheese straws, and so on do not present any problems — except they are generally high in fat. Unfortunately, this is the case with most party fare. Provided some low-fat goodies like jelly and fresh fruit (or fruit salad), are provided to reduce the total fat content of the meal, there is no need to be too worried on this score provided you do not party often.

It is the sweet treats that can be particularly troublesome, so I have concentrated on providing this type of recipe here. Luckily, as children get older, savoury dishes generally gain greater acceptability. This makes planning parties somewhat easier.

Don't forget that at least half the fun of a party is getting ready. Let your children do as much food preparation as possible to foster an enjoyment of cooking. It can be great fun.

Refer to the section on cake decorating for suggestions for titivating cakes for birthdays and other special occasions.

# Gingerbread Men

**Dairy free if dairy-free margarine used instead of butter**

2 tablespoons golden syrup
1½ cups flour
¾ cup ground rice
3 teaspoons ground ginger
1 teaspoon bicarbonate of soda
100g butter
1 egg
1 tablespoon liquid artificial sweetener (equivalent to ½ cup sugar)
2 tablespoons water (approximately)

For decoration: pumpkin and sunflower seeds, long thread coconut, dried apricots (chopped), currants

First, warm the golden syrup. I just stand the golden syrup tin in hot water and proceed with the mixing. Place all the dry ingredients into a food processor with butter, and blend until mixture resembles fine crumbs. Add egg, artificial sweetener and warmed golden syrup, and blend to mix. Next, add water one tablespoon at a time, blending well after each addition, until the mixture forms a dough which presses together easily. Roll dough out to 0.5cm thickness and cut out gingerbread men. If you do not have a special cutter, just make a cardboard model to cut around. I find the size and shape drawn below very practical to handle and decorate. Place cut out gingerbread men on to greased oven tray and have fun decorating them with, for example: sunflower seed eyes, pumpkin seed hands and feet, dried apricot mouth, long thread coconut hair, currant nose and buttons down front. I find brushing the 'men' lightly with water just before decorating helps the decorations stick fast. Bake 15 minutes at 180ºC (350ºF).

*Makes 20 gingerbread men*

*Each gingerbread man (undecorated) provides approximately:*
1½ **CARBOHYDRATE CHOICES, 1 FAT & OIL CHOICE,**

*14g carbohydrate, 2g protein, 4.5g fat, 0.6g dietary fibre, 110 kcal (450 kJ)*

# Chocolate Crackles

100g *vegetable shortening*
3 *tablespoons cocoa*
¼ *cup ground rice*
¼ *cup non-fat milk powder*
½ *cup coconut*
4 *sachets aspartame sweetener (equivalent to 3 tablespoons sugar)*
2 *cups rice bubbles*

Melt vegetable shortening. Add cocoa and ground rice and stir until lump free. Add non-fat milk powder and coconut and mix in. Then add aspartame sweetener and mix to disperse. Lastly, add rice bubbles and mix to distribute through chocolate coating. Spoon mixture into paper patty pans and refrigerate to set.

**Makes 24 chocolate crackles**

**Each chocolate crackle provides approximately:**
**½ CARBOHYDRATE CHOICE, 1 FAT & OIL CHOICE,**
**4.5g carbohydrate, 0.9g protein, 5.5g fat, 0.5g dietary fibre, 69 kcal (290 kJ)**

# Strawberry Marshmallow Shortcake

A brightly coloured treat enjoyed by the young and the not-so-young!

Note: *Evaporated milk must be chilled thoroughly to make topping.*

### Base

2 cups flour
1 teaspoon baking powder
½ cup coconut
75g butter
2 egg yolks
1 tablespoon liquid artificial sweetener (equivalent to ½ cup sugar)
3 tablespoons cold water

### Marshmallow Topping

1 sachet low-calorie strawberry jelly mix (usually used to make 500ml jelly)
¼ cup water
¾ cup evaporated milk, well chilled
2 egg whites
¼ cup coconut

To make base, place flour, baking powder, and coconut in blender with butter and blend until butter rubbed through dry ingredients. Add egg yolks and artificial sweetener and blend to mix. Finally add water and blend to form dough. Press evenly into base of sponge roll tin. Bake for 15-20 minutes at 180ºC (350ºF). Cool.

To make the marshmallow topping, sprinkle jelly mix over water in a saucepan. Heat while stirring until jelly mix dissolves. Set aside to cool. Beat evaporated milk until stiff. Add dissolved jelly mix to egg whites and whip until frothy. Then fold this mixture gently through the whipped evaporated milk. Spread over base quickly because the chilled milk speeds up setting. Sprinkle coconut over the surface of the topping. Once set, cut into 24 squares. Store in refrigerator.

---

*Makes 24 squares*

*Each serving provides approximately:*
**1 CARBOHYDRATE CHOICE, ½ PROTEIN CHOICE, ½ FAT & OIL CHOICE,**
**9.5g carbohydrate, 3g protein, 5.5g fat, 1g dietary fibre, 100 kcal (410 kJ)**

---

# Pizza Faces

Pizza is always popular, but I find mini-pizzas are best for children's parties as they can be easily managed by small fingers. Arranging toppings to produce faces adds extra interest (this is a fun task for the children).

The recipe given here for the tomato filling makes more than is required for a dozen pizza faces. Use the balance to make a pizza for the adults, or freeze for future use.

### Tomato Filling
2 *teaspoons vegetable oil*
1 *clove garlic, crushed*
1 *onion, finely sliced*
2 *rashers bacon, cut into small pieces*
400g *can whole peeled tomatoes*
2 *tablespoons tomato paste*
½ *teaspoon basil*
½ *teaspoon oreganum*
*freshly ground black pepper*

### Scone Crust
¾ *cup flour*
¾ *cup wholemeal flour*
2 *teaspoons baking powder*
1 *tablespoon butter*
½ *cup water (approximately)*

### Toppings
1 *cup grated tasty Cheddar cheese, lightly packed (80g)*
6 *pineapple pieces in unsweetened fruit juice, drained and sliced in half*
1 *bier stick, sliced finely*
1 *tomato, cut into small wedges*

To make tomato filling, heat oil in saucepan. Saute garlic, onion and bacon in oil until onion is tender and light in colour. Add whole peeled tomatoes (undrained), tomato paste, basil, oreganum and freshly ground black pepper to taste. Break up whole tomatoes with wooden spoon, bring to the boil then simmer until mixture reduces to a thick sauce (about 15-20 minutes). This recipe makes approximately 1⅔ cups of filling of which only approximately ⅓ cup is required for preparation of these faces.

Prepare scone crust while tomato filling reduces. Place flours, baking powder and butter in a mixing bowl and rub butter through the dry ingredients until the mixture resembles fine breadcrumbs. Form a well in centre of these dry ingredients and pour the water into it. Mix to form a stiff dough, adding a little more water if necessary to achieve desired consistency. Turn dough out on to a lightly floured board and knead lightly. Roll out to approximately 0.5cm thick. Cut 12 rounds of pastry using a large round biscuit cutter. Place rounds on greased oven tray and top with a rounded teaspoon of tomato filling.

Lastly apply the toppings. Sprinkle grated cheese evenly over 12 rounds, then decorate each one with two bier stick slice eyes, a pineapple nose and a smiley tomato-wedge mouth. Bake at 180ºC (350ºF) until cheese is melted and bubbly, about 15 minutes. Serve warm.

---

*Makes 12 pizza faces*

*Each pizza serving provides approximately:*
1½ **CARBOHYDRATE CHOICES, 1 PROTEIN CHOICE,**
*14g carbohydrate, 5.5g protein, 6g fat, 1.5 g dietary fibre, 130 kcal (540 kJ)*

---

# Orange Boats

**Dairy free**

4 teaspoons gelatine
¼ cup water
4 oranges
juice of 2 lemons
1 egg, separated
6 sachets aspartame sweetener (equivalent to ¼ cup sugar)

bamboo skewers for masts and coloured cardboard for sails

Sprinkle gelatine over water in a saucepan and leave to stand.
Halve oranges, remove pips, then remove pulp without breaking
the rinds. Rub the pulp through a sieve. Heat the water and
gelatine, while stirring, until gelatine dissolves, then add to orange
pulp along with lemon juice, egg yolk and sweetener. Whisk until
combined. Finally fold in the stiffly beaten egg white and spoon
into the orange cases. Refrigerate until set, then add mast and
sails. Cut long bamboo skewers in half to make the masts, and
cut sails out of coloured cardboard. A square pirate sail is the
easiest; simply thread the mast through a central hole near the
bottom of the sail, and then through another central hole near
the top. Children can have great fun making and decorating the
sails. Putting names on the sails can be a fun way of organising
place settings. Alternatively, serve boats regatta-style on one large
plate.

*Makes 8 orange boats*

*Each boat provides approximately:*
*½ CARBOHYDRATE CHOICE,*
*4g carbohydrate, 2.5g protein, 0.7g fat, 31 kcal (130 kJ)*

# CAKE DECORATING: GLAZES, TOPPINGS AND FILLINGS

Decorating cakes for birthdays or other festive occasions can require extra creative skill! Uniced cakes can be made to look interesting by baking them in different-shaped cake tins, for example a tin the shape of the appropriate number for the child's age, a gingerbread man, a heart shape, etc. These are usually available for hire from cake shops in larger towns or cities. Cakes can be decorated with chopped nuts or seeds before baking. Alternatively, or in addition to this type of decoration, inedible accessories like cocktail flags and small toys can be used. Paper borders can be made to wrap around the outside of a cake, and decorated as you please.

This section includes a number of low-fat soft cheese based glaze recipes which are FREE (or very nearly), plus a higher fat nutty carob topping, which can all be used as icing substitutes. I have purposely kept this section quite separate from the cake section, because cakes do not need to be glazed as a matter of course. All these icing substitutes (FREE or not) add extra calories per serving. Never glaze down the sides of cakes – doing the top surface alone adds enough extra calories! Once a cake is glazed, it needs to be stored in a refrigerator.

There are endless ways these glazes can be decorated – try using coconut (colour by toasting, or with food colouring if desired); dried fruits; pumpkin, sunflower and sesame seeds; walnut halves or pieces; almonds and other nuts; fresh fruit like strawberry halves or orange segments.

When it comes to preparing cakes for festive occasions there are many novel things you can do. Making a steamed pudding, for instance the Chocolate Steamed Pudding (see recipe p. 97) can provide a different shape to work with. Cutting a hole in the centre to allow a small doll to be inserted to the waist can enable you to create an exotic ball-gown design. Ring cakes can be cut in half and rejoined to produce a worm or train shape. Ice-Cream cakes (see Ice-Cream recipe p. 112) can be set in many different-shaped moulds (and what is more they need little titivating – just a little whipped cream).

The Light Cream Filling recipe included in this section is FREE and very adaptable. It can be used to fill cakes, muffins, patty cakes, choux pastry cases or what ever takes your fancy.

# Nutty Carob Topping

**Dairy free**

This interesting topping, made from a base of rolled oats, peanut butter and dates, can be modified readily to produce different flavoured toppings. For example, to make a carob and orange flavoured topping, add the grated rind of 1 orange and substitute orange juice for water. Note the high fat content though, and only use occasionally.

½ cup rolled oats
¼ cup peanut butter
6 pitted dates
1 tablespoon carob powder
1 tablespoon dry sherry
3 tablespoons water (approximately)

Place all ingredients in food processor. Blend until rolled oats broken up and ingredients combined. If topping is too thick to spread or press out, blend in a little extra water.

*Makes approximately 1 cup; sufficient to spread over top surface of a cake cooked in a ring tin, or in a 20 x 20cm cake tin.*

*When divided between 20 servings, adds per serving:*
*½ FAT & OIL CHOICE,*
*3g carbohydrate, 1g protein, 2g fat, 0.6g dietary fibre, 35 kcal (150 kJ)*

# Chocolate Yoghurt Glaze

2 tablespoons cold water
2 tablespoons cocoa
150g low-fat soft cheese
¼ cup unsweetened low-fat natural yoghurt
3 sachets aspartame sweetener (equivalent to 2 tablespoons sugar)
1 teaspoon vanilla essence

Place water and cocoa in a small saucepan and heat while stirring until a thick smooth paste has been attained. Remove from heat. In a bowl beat the low-fat soft cheese vigorously until it has a creamy lump-free consistency. Add the cocoa paste and mix through. Add the remaining ingredients and mix until combined. Use immediately to glaze chocolate cake (or other cake of your choice). Spread evenly over top surface of cake, then smooth with the flat edge of a knife, or make swirling patterns with a knife or fork to give a textured surface.

*Makes approximately 1 cup; sufficient to glaze the top surface of a ring cake, or a cake cooked in a 20 x 20cm cake tin.*

*When divided between 20 servings, adds per serving:*
*1.5g carbohydrate, 1g protein, 0.8g fat, 16 kcal (67 kJ)*

Note: This is just slightly too high in calories to qualify as a free food.

# Vanilla Soft-Cheese Glaze

¼ cup Trim milk
2 teaspoons cornflour
150g low-fat soft cheese
3 sachets aspartame sweetener (equivalent to 2 tablespoons sugar)
½ teaspoon vanilla essence

Mix milk and cornflour together in a small saucepan until smooth.
Heat until thickened, stirring constantly. Remove from heat. Cream
low-fat soft cheese until smooth, then mix cornflour paste through
it. Lastly, add sweetener and vanilla essence and mix thoroughly.
Use immediately; spread over top surface of cake, then smooth
off or texture surface using a knife.

**Makes approximately 1 cup; sufficient to glaze the top surface of a
ring cake, or a cake cooked in a 20 x 20cm cake tin.**

**When divided between 20 servings, adds per serving:
1.5g carbohydrate, 0.8g protein, 0.6g fat, 15 kcal (61 kJ)**

Note: This is just slightly too high in calories too qualify as a free food.

# Lemon Soft-Cheese Glaze

This is delicious on carrot and banana cakes.

Make as for vanilla soft-cheese glaze above, omitting vanilla, and replacing milk with the grated rind of 1 lemon, plus the juice of 1 lemon made up to ¼ cup volume with water. Use 4 rather than 3 sachets aspartame sweetener (equivalent to 3 tablespoons sugar).

*Makes approximately 1 cup; sufficient to glaze the top surface of a ring cake, or a cake cooked in a 20 x 20cm cake tin.*

**FREE FOOD**
*When divided between 20 servings, adds per serving:*
*1.5g carbohydrate, 0.7g protein, 0.6g fat, 14 kcal (57 kJ)*

# Light Cream Filling

This simple filling can be used for cakes, muffins, cup cakes, choux pastry cases, etc. Use in conjunction with fresh berries or other fruit, or add a little fruit pulp to filling for variety, for example filling for Peaches and Cream Muffins (see recipe p. 46).

*½ cup low-fat sour cream*
*1 sachet aspartame sweetener (equivalent to 2 teaspoons sugar)*
*¼ teaspoon vanilla essence*

Simply mix all the ingredients together and it is ready to use.

*Makes approximately ½ cup*

*1 serving = 1 teaspoon*
**FREE FOOD**
*0.4g carbohydrate, 0.3g protein, 0.6g fat, 8 kcal (34 kJ)*

# SWEETS AND TREATS

More recipes to enrich special occasions. Once again, please note that these are high-fat recipes, meant for the occasional indulgence only. Make these recipes when you are having a few people round, or when you are going to someone else's place, so most of what is made disappears quickly and you are not left with a pile of temptation.

## Nut and Raisin Chocolate

Make as for chocolate (see recipe p. 131) but add these extra ingredients to the mix:

⅓ *cup coconut*
½ *cup raisins*
½ *cup peanuts*

Cut into 25 pieces, again preferably before the chocolate sets very hard.

*Makes 25 servings*

*Each serving provides approximately:*
½ CARBOHYDRATE CHOICE, 1½ FAT & OIL CHOICES,
*5g carbohydrate, 1.5g protein, 6.5g fat, 0.7g dietary fibre, 83 kcal (340 kJ)*

# Chocolate

Most chocolate recipes tend to be very high in fat, and tend to include high amounts of non-fat milk powder, which contains almost 50% of the simple sugar lactose. This recipe is still high in fat, but the proportion of non-fat milk powder has been reduced by using it in conjunction with ground rice. Replacing all the non-fat milk powder with ground rice gives a gritty mouth-feel, but when used together the texture is very satisfactory.

100g vegetable shortening
3 tablespoons cocoa
1 teaspoon vanilla essence
⅓ cup ground rice
⅓ cup non-fat milk powder
4 sachets aspartame sweetener (equivalent to 3 tablespoons of sugar)

Melt vegetable shortening. Add cocoa, vanilla and ground rice, and stir until lump-free. Add non-fat milk powder and mix. Lastly, add aspartame sweetener and mix well. Adding the heat sensitive aspartame sweetener last is a simple precaution — it allows the hot vegetable shortening to be cooled by the addition of the other ingredients. Pour mixture into shallow tray (a 2 litre plastic ice-cream container is a suitable size), and refrigerate to set. Cut into 20 pieces, preferably before the chocolate sets very hard.

---

**Makes 20 servings**

**Each serving provides approximately:**
**1 FAT & OIL CHOICE,**
**3.5g carbohydrate, 1g protein, 5g fat, 65 kcal (270 kJ)**

---

# Jaffa Balls

### Dairy free

These truffle-like balls are lovely to serve with coffee at the conclusion of a special meal.

½ cup coconut, toasted
½ cup rolled oats, toasted (toast just as for coconut)
¼ cup peanut butter
¼ cup sultanas
1 tablespoon cocoa
rind of 1 orange
3 tablespoons orange juice
2 sachets aspartame sweetener (equivalent to 4 teaspoons sugar)

Mix all the ingredients together. Using hands, take small amounts of mixture, press and roll into balls. Store in refrigerator.

*Makes 12 balls*

*Each ball provides approximately*:
**½ CARBOHYDRATE CHOICE, 1 FAT & OIL CHOICE,**
**6g carbohydrate, 2g protein, 5g fat, 1.5g dietary fibre, 78 kcal (320 kJ)**

# Nutty Carob Balls

**Dairy free**

Toasted nuts, seeds and rolled oats form the basis of these tasty little balls. I often make these at Easter time when everyone else is indulging in Easter eggs.

½ cup walnut pieces (50g)
1¼ cups rolled oats
⅓ cup sunflower seeds
⅓ cup sesame seeds
½ cup raisins
1 tablespoon carob powder
grated rind of 1 orange
juice of 1 orange made up to ¼ cup with water
1 tablespoon dry sherry
½ teaspoon cinnamon

Spread walnuts, rolled oats and seeds thinly over base of a shallow oven dish and toast in the oven until golden brown, approximately 10 minutes at 160°C (325°F). Transfer these toasted ingredients to a food processor and blend until they are ground to a coarse powder. Remove from food processor. Place all the other ingredients in the food processor and blend until mixed, and raisins are partially broken into small pieces. Gradually add the dry toasted ingredients to this mixture, while blending. Stop blending when all the ingredients are combined. Press dough together and divide into 3 equal-sized pieces. Cut each of these pieces into 8 equal-sized segments and shape these into balls. Store in refrigerator.

*Makes 24 balls*

*Each ball provides approximately*:
½ **CARBOHYDRATE CHOICE**, ½ **FAT & OIL CHOICE**,
*6g carbohydrate, 1.5g protein, 3.5g fat, 0.9g dietary fibre, 60 kcal (250 kJ)*

# Chocolate Fudge Cake

A popular indulgence for all age groups.

## Biscuit Base

250g wine biscuits, finely crushed
1 cup coconut (for added interest use long thread coconut instead of standard fine or medium)
½ cup sultanas
100g butter
2 eggs, lightly beaten
3 tablespoons cocoa
1 teaspoon vanilla essence
4 sachets aspartame sweetener (equivalent to 3 tablespoons sugar)

## Topping

75g vegetable shortening
¼ cup non-fat milk powder
¼ cup ground rice
⅓ cup cocoa
½ teaspoon vanilla essence
4 sachets aspartame sweetener (equivalent to 3 tablespoons sugar)

To make biscuit base, place crushed wine biscuits, coconut and sultanas in a bowl and mix. Melt butter over low heat in a small saucepan. Remove from heat to add and mix in eggs. Heat gently, while stirring, until this mixture starts to thicken (*do not boil*). Remove from heat. Add cocoa and mix in. Then add vanilla and sweetener and mix to combine. Pour over dry ingredients in bowl and mix through. I find the best way to do this is to use my fingers. Press this mixture very firmly into a 20 x 20cm tin. Refrigerate while preparing topping.

Melt vegetable shortening on low heat. Remove from heat and stir in non-fat milk powder, ground rice and cocoa. Lastly stir in vanilla and sweetener. Pour over biscuit base and spread out evenly. Refrigerate to set. Cut into 36 squares, preferably before chocolate topping sets very hard. Store in refrigerator.

*Makes 36 squares*

*Each square provides approximately*:
1 CARBOHYDRATE CHOICE, 1½ FAT & OIL CHOICES,
*8.5g carbohydrate, 2g protein, 7g fat, 0.6g dietary fibre, 100 kcal
(430 kJ)*

# CHRISTMAS AND EASTER FARE

## White Christmas

This is an adaptation of a Christmas treat that my mother made when I was a child.

100g *vegetable shortening*
¼ *cup non-fat milk powder*
¼ *cup ground rice*
⅓ *cup coconut*
⅓ *cup sunflower seeds*
⅓ *cup pumpkin seeds*
3 *sachets aspartame sweetener (equivalent to 2 tablespoons sugar)*
⅓ *cup raisins*
4 *dried apricots, finely chopped*
⅓ *cup rice bubbles*

Melt vegetable shortening. Add non-fat milk powder and ground rice, and stir until lump-free. Add sunflower and pumpkin seeds and mix. By this stage the mixture should be sufficiently cool to add aspartame sweetener: add and mix to disperse. Add rest of ingredients, mix and pour into shallow tray. Refrigerate to set. When almost set, cut into 25 pieces, then refrigerate again to set hard.

*Makes 25 pieces*

*Each piece provides approximately:*
½ **CARBOHYDRATE CHOICE,** 1½ **FAT & OIL CHOICES,**
**4.5g carbohydrate, 1.5g protein, 6.5g fat, 0.7g dietary fibre, 81 kcal (340 kJ)**

# Orange Brandy Custard

This is an inspired variation of the more traditional brandy sauce or custard accompaniment for Christmas pudding.

*grated rind of ½ orange*
*juice of 1 orange made up to ⅓ cup with water*
*2 egg yolks*
*2 tablespoons brandy*
*4 sachets aspartame sweetener (equivalent to 3 tablespoons sugar)*
*¼ cup cream, whipped*

Place orange rind and juice, and egg yolks in a small saucepan and whisk together. Heat over medium heat, while constantly stirring, until the mix starts to thicken. Remove from heat. Add brandy, mix in, then add sweetener and mix again. Finally fold the custard mixture through the whipped cream and it is ready to serve.

**Makes 8 servings, approximately 1 cup**

**1 serving = 2 tablespoons**
**1 FAT & OIL CHOICE,**
**1.5g carbohydrate, 1g protein, 4.5g fat, 0.1g dietary fibre, 59 kcal (250 kJ)**

*Note: If you prefer to follow tradition, omit orange rind and replace orange juice with ⅓ cup water – this makes a superb brandy custard.*

# Christmas Cake

**Dairy free if dairy-free margarine used instead of butter**

This is the Christmas cake I have made for the last few years. The dried fruit is soaked in whisky and fruit juices for 3-4 weeks before the cake is made, giving it a very rich flavour. I usually prepare the fruit in early November and bake the cake in early December. This allows time for the flavours to mingle before Christmas. As this is a large cake, once cut at Christmas time, I generally freeze half of it, in 2 separate pieces, for enjoyment later in the summer, or for Easter.

700g sultanas
700g raisins
280g currants
170g dates, pitted and chopped
100g prunes, stoned and chopped
grated rind of 2 lemons
juice of 2 lemons made up to ¼ cup with water
grated rind of 2 oranges
juice of 2 oranges made up to ½ cup with water
1 green apple, cored and grated
⅔ cup whisky
185g butter
1 cup freshly brewed tea
100g walnuts, chopped
70g ground almonds
4 eggs, lightly beaten
3 cups flour
2 teaspoons baking powder
1 teaspoon cinnamon
½ teaspoon nutmeg
2 tablespoons whisky, extra

Place dried fruit, citrus rinds and juices, grated apple and ⅔ cup whisky in a large screw-top jar, or large well-sealing plastic container. Shake to mix ingredients. Store 3-4 weeks in a cool, dry place, shaking or inverting container every 2-3 days. Transfer fruit to a very large mixing bowl. Melt butter and add to fruit with hot tea. Add nuts, eggs and dry ingredients. Mix well until a uniform mixture is obtained. Transfer mixture to a prepared (base lined with greaseproof paper and greased) 23 x 23cm deep cake tin. Decorate surface with whole or split almonds if desired (see ideas on cake decorations p. 125). Bake in a slow oven (150-160°C (300-325°F) until cooked, usually 2¾-3½ hours. Remove from oven, brush evenly with extra whisky. Cover with aluminium foil and leave in tin until cold. Remove from tin, remove greaseproof from base, then wrap up well in greaseproof paper. Store in a cool dry place until Christmas.

---

*Makes 1 large cake*

**Divided into 80 equal servings, each serving provides approximately:**
**2 CARBOHYDRATE CHOICES, ½ FAT & OIL CHOICE,**
**20g carbohydrate, 1.5g protein, 3.5g fat, 2.5g dietary fibre, 120 kcal (500 kJ)**
**HIGH-FRUIT RECIPE**

*Note: To help get correct serving sizes, cut into quarters first, then cut each quarter into 20 servings.*

---

# Quick Mix Christmas Cake

**Dairy free if dairy-free margarine used instead of butter**

For those of you who do not want a large cake, or cannot be bothered with the advanced organisation required to make the previous recipe, here is a smaller quick-mix alternative. The light colour of this cake belies its rich blend of flavours. Use brandy instead of dry sherry if you prefer a brandy flavour.

300g sultanas
250g currants
200g raisins
1 Granny Smith apple, peeled and grated
¼ cup dry sherry
grated rind of 1 orange
juice of 1 orange made up to ¼ cup with water
⅔ cup water
75g butter
1 cup wholemeal flour
1 cup flour
2 teaspoons baking powder
1 teaspoon mixed spice
2 eggs

Place sultanas, currants, raisins and grated apple in a large mixing bowl, then add sherry. In a small saucepan heat together the orange rind and juice, water and butter, until butter is melted. Pour over fruit, then break up any large clumps of fruit with a wooden spoon. Add dry ingredients and eggs, and mix well to combine. Transfer cake mix to prepared (base lined with greaseproof paper and greased) 20 x 20cm cake tin. Bake at 160°C (325°F) until cooked, approximately 1½ hours.

*Makes 1 cake*

*Divided into 64 equal servings, each serving provides approximately:*
**1 CARBOHYDRATE CHOICE,**

**11g carbohydrate, 1g protein, 1g fat, 1g dietary fibre, 58 kcal (250 kJ)**
## HIGH-FRUIT RECIPE

Note: To help to get correct serving sizes, cut cake into quarters first, then cut each quarter into 16 pieces.

Another choice is Celebration Cake (see recipe p. 70) which is as befitting Christmas as any other special occasion.

# Fruit Mince Slice

**Dairy free if dairy-free margarine used instead of butter**

This fruit mince recipe could equally well be used to make fruit mince pies, but I find it much less time consuming to make one large slice than lots of little pies.

## Pastry
3 cups flour
100g butter
1 egg
2 teaspoons liquid artificial sweetener (equivalent to ¼ cup sugar)
⅓-½ cup water

## Fruit Mince
430g can crushed pineapple in unsweetened pineapple juice
1 cup sultanas
1 cup raisins
½ cup currants
1 apple, peeled, cored and grated
grated rind of 1 lemon
½ teaspoon cinnamon
½ teaspoon nutmeg
1 tablespoon cornflour
¼ cup brandy

To make pastry, place flour and butter in a food processor and blend until the butter is rubbed through the flour. Add egg and sweetener, and blend to combine. Add ⅓ cup of water and blend thoroughly. If a dough does not form, add extra water 1 tablespoon at a time, blending after each addition, until a dough that clumps together is achieved. Wrap dough in plastic film and refrigerate for 45 minutes – you can use some of this time to make the fruit mince (see below) and then leave it to cool. Roll out half of the pastry and use it to line a sponge roll tin. Fill with cooled fruit mince. Brush edges of pastry lightly with water. Roll out remaining pastry, place in position over filling, then pinch edges of both layers of pastry together. Prick the top layer of pastry generously with a fork. Bake for 10 minutes at 200°C (400°F), reduce heat to 180°C

(350°F) and cook a further 15 minutes. When cool, cut into 24 squares.

To make the fruit mince, combine all the ingredients, except the cornflour and brandy, in a saucepan. Stir over medium heat until the mixture boils, then reduce heat and simmer for 3 minutes. Blend cornflour and brandy to a smooth paste and add to the hot fruit mixture. Stir until mixture boils and thickens. Cool.

---

*Makes 24 squares*

*Each square provides approximately*:
2½ CARBOHYDRATE CHOICES, 1 FAT & OIL CHOICE,
*26g carbohydrate, 2.5g protein, 4g fat, 2.5g dietary fibre, 150 kcal (650 kJ)*

HIGH-FRUIT RECIPE

---

# Christmas Pudding

**Dairy free**

Traditional Christmas puddings are packed so densely with dried fruits that serving sizes of 2, or even 3-4 CARBOHYDRATE CHOICES are very small indeed. People generally expect rich fruit cakes to be cut into small pieces, but do not so readily accept meagre portions of pudding. This recipe is lighter than traditional Christmas puddings for this reason. While it still provides 16 servings of 2 CARBOHYDRATE CHOICES each, I would expect it to serve only 10-12 people (assuming most of these people are not diabetic).

⅓ cup each raisins, sultanas and currants
1 cup grated carrot, lightly packed (90g)
½ cup grated apple, lightly packed (50g)
½ cup chopped walnuts
¼ cup brandy
grated rind of 2 oranges
juice of 2 oranges made up to ½ cup with water
⅓ cup water
1 cup flour
1 cup wholemeal flour
1 teaspoon baking powder
1 teaspoon bicarbonate of soda
1 teaspoon cinnamon
1 teaspoon mixed spice
¼ teaspoon nutmeg
2 eggs
¼ cup vegetable oil

Place dried fruit, grated carrot and apple, and chopped walnuts in a large mixing bowl. Add brandy, orange rind and juice, and water. Add dry ingredients, eggs and oil, and mix well to combine. Transfer mixture into a well-greased pudding bowl of at least 5 cup (1.25 litre) capacity. Cover and steam for 2½ hours. Serve warm with Orange Brandy Custard (see recipe p. 137).

If you wish to minimise preparation required on Christmas day, leave fruits soaking in brandy, orange rind and juice and water overnight. Also measure out dry ingredients and prepare bowl ahead of time.

---

*Makes* 1 *large pudding*

**Divided into** 16 *equal servings, each serving provides approximately:*
**2 CARBOHYDRATE CHOICES, ½ PROTEIN CHOICE, ½ FAT &
OIL CHOICE,**
**20g** *carbohydrate,* **3.5g** *protein,* **4.5g** *fat,* **2.5g** *dietary fibre,* **140 kcal
(600 kJ)**

**HIGH-FRUIT RECIPE**

---

# Hot Cross Buns

### Dairy free

Yeast cookery is always fun but there is something especially satisfying about making your own hot cross buns at Easter. This recipe makes 30 small buns. This may sound a lot, but with yeast cookery it takes very little extra time to make a large recipe compared to a small one. Freeze excess buns for your pleasure at a later date.

The bun size needs to be kept on the small side otherwise the dried fruit added pushes the total carbohydrate content of each bun up too high. The cracked wheat in this recipe gives these buns a slightly nutty flavour, which blends deliciously with the spice and fruit flavours. No sugar is added because there are sufficient natural sugars present from the fruit juices and fruit to sustain the yeast. The salt is needed for a satisfactory end result.

## Buns
½ cup cracked wheat
¾ cup cold water
1 cup unsweetened apple juice
2 tablespoons active dried yeast
1 teaspoon salt
¼ cup vegetable oil
1 egg, slightly beaten
rind of 1 orange
juice of 1 orange made up to ¼ cup with water
rind of 1 lemon
juice of 1 lemon made up to ¼ cup with water
¾ cup sultanas
1 teaspoon cinnamon
2 teaspoons mixed spice
3 cups wholemeal flour
3 cups flour

## Batter for Crosses
⅓ cup water
⅓ cup flour

Heat cracked wheat in cold water, simmer for 10 minutes, then allow to cool. Heat apple juice until blood temperature. Place in a large warm mixing bowl, dissolve the yeast in this, then add the cracked wheat (undrained) and all the other ingredients except the flour. Add 1½ cups of each type of flour and beat very, very well. Add almost all of the remaining flour, ½ cup of each at a time, mixing each additional lot of flour into dough before adding any more. Turn dough on to a lightly floured board and knead for 5-10 minutes until dough is smooth and satiny. Add the reserved flour if necessary to avoid sticking. Place dough in a warm, well-oiled bowl. Place bowl in a large plastic bag, and leave it in a warm place until it doubles in bulk.

Punch dough down and knead lightly in the bowl for about a minute. Divide dough into 30 equal pieces. Shape each piece into a roll. Place rolls close together, but not touching (to allow room for rising), in greased cake tin(s) or on a greased oven tray. Put back in large plastic bag(s) and return to a warm place. Leave to rise until doubled in size again.

Make a smooth paste from ⅓ cup flour and ⅓ cup of cold water, adding more water, or flour, as required to give a suitable consistency for piping. Pipe crosses on to buns using this batter. If you do not have a piping device use a small plastic bag with one corner snipped off. Place batter in bag, secure top, and squeeze batter out of cut corner. Bake buns for 20 minutes at 190°C (375°F). Serve warm.

---

**Makes 30 buns**

**1 serving = 1 bun**
**2½ CARBOHYDRATE CHOICES, ½ PROTEIN CHOICE,**
**26g carbohydrate, 4.5g protein, 2.5g fat, 3g dietary fibre, 140 kcal (600 kJ)**

---

# Easter Nests

Here is a simple way to make a special Easter Sunday surprise. You could alternatively mould your own Easter eggs using the Chocolate recipe (see p. 67), but making a nest is much quicker and easier.

20g vegetable shortening
1 teaspoon cocoa
2-3 drops vanilla essence
1 tablespoon ground rice
1 tablespoon non-fat milk powder
1 sachet aspartame sweetener (equivalent to 2 teaspoons sugar)
1 tablespoon long thread coconut
1 tablespoon rice bubbles
1 tablespoon raisins
1 tablespoon long thread coconut, extra
Easter chicken(s) (inedible)

Melt vegetable shortening in a small saucepan, then remove from heat. Add cocoa and vanilla essence, and mix until lump-free. Next add ground rice and milk powder, and mix again. Finally add sweetener, long thread coconut, rice bubbles and raisins, and mix to combine. Pour this chocolate mix into the bottom of a small dessert plate. Sprinkle extra long thread coconut over surface. Then get a glass and press it into centre of 'nest' to create a depression, but not so far that it goes right through. Refrigerate with glass on top until chocolate is almost set. Remove glass before it gets stuck hard into chocolate, then refrigerate 'nest' again until set hard. To remove 'nest' from dessert plate, sit bottom of plate in hot water for about 30 seconds to melt bottom edge of chocolate, then slip nest out. Store in refrigerator until required. Sit Easter chicken(s) on top.

**Makes 1 nest**

**Once nest has been discovered, cut into eight equal pieces for gradual consumption. Each of these 8 servings provides approximately:**
**½ FAT & OIL CHOICE,**
**2.5g carbohydrate, 0.5g protein, 3g fat, 0.3g dietary fibre, 41 kcal (170 kJ)**

# VEGETABLE DISHES, SALADS AND SALAD DRESSINGS

For good nutrition you should include a wide variety of vegetables (both raw and cooked) in your diet, and eat plenty of them. They are generally low in fat and high in fibre. Starchy vegetables like potatoes, kumera and parsnip are excellent sources of complex carbohydrates.

Summer salads made from fresh raw vegetables create mental images of healthy eating, but they are not so good for you if they are drowned with high-fat dressings. Classical French dressing made from 3-4 parts oil to 1 part vinegar, wine or lemon juice, is very high in fat. When making vinaigrette dressings I use equal amounts of oil and vinegar and bulk out the dressing by adding herbs or other low-fat ingredients like tomato pulp. As a general rule, try to make dressings with lots of flavour and pep, so only minimal quantities need to be added to salads to achieve the desired flavour enhancement.

For maximum retention of nutrients, cook vegetables by steaming, or boiling in a minimal amount of water, until just cooked through. Avoid frying and roasting vegetables because they absorb tremendous amounts of fat when cooked this way. Rich sauces served with vegetables do not help the waistline either. Instead, add interest to vegetables by including extra flavourings in the cooking liquor, for example crushed garlic with beans, or a little orange peel and cinnamon with carrots. Serve vegetables in interesting combinations as hot or cold salads, or use to add colour, flavour and bulk to meat dishes.

The two vegetable slice recipes included here can be used as main or side dishes. They are similar to quiches except they do not have any calorific pastry round the outside. To ensure you get a good crust on these slices, grease the baking dish well, then lightly sprinkle a little flour over the surface before adding mix.

This section includes just a few vegetable and salad recipes which I hope you will enjoy.

# Courgette Slice

375g courgettes
2 medium onions, finely chopped
3 lean rashers bacon, finely cut
1 cup grated tasty Cheddar cheese, lightly packed (80g)
1 cup flour
1 teaspoon baking powder
4 eggs
1 cup Trim milk
salt and pepper to taste

Grate unpeeled courgettes coarsely, and place in a large mixing bowl. Add all the rest of the ingredients to the grated courgette and mix thoroughly. Pour mixture into greased and lightly floured, round 23cm ovenproof dish. Bake at 180°C (350°F) for 35-40 minutes, or until browned and set.

**Makes 1 slice**

**Divided into 8 equal servings, each serving provides approximately:
2 CARBOHYDRATE CHOICES, 2 PROTEIN CHOICES,
18g carbohydrate, 14g protein, 8.5g fat, 1.5g dietary fibre, 200 kcal
(850 kJ)**

# Spinach Slice

200g spinach (or silverbeet), washed well, stalks removed
1 cup grated tasty Cheddar cheese, lightly packed (80g)
1 large onion, finely chopped
1 clove garlic, crushed
3 lean rashers bacon, finely cut
1 cup wholemeal flour
1 teaspoon baking powder
250g low-fat cottage cheese
4 eggs
1 cup Trim milk
salt and pepper to taste

Blend spinach to a pulp in 2 or more batches, depending on the size of your food processor. Transfer pulped spinach to a large mixing bowl. Add all the other ingredients to the spinach and mix very well. Transfer mixture into a greased and lightly floured, round 23cm ovenproof dish. Bake at 180°C (350°F) for 35-40 minutes, or until browned and set.

**Makes 1 slice**

**Divided into 8 equal servings, each serving provides approximately:
1½ CARBOHYDRATE CHOICES, 2½ PROTEIN CHOICES,
17g carbohydrate, 19g protein, 8.5g fat, 3g dietary fibre, 220 kcal
(930 kJ)**

# Tomato and Onion Stuffed Marrow

This tasty recipe is especially for people (like us) who grow courgettes and every so often accidentally let one grow to gigantic proportions.

3 *medium-sized tomatoes*
1 *onion, peeled*
1 *clove garlic, peeled*
*salt and pepper*
2 *slices wholegrain bread*
1 *tablespoon butter*
½ *large marrow (cut lengthwise), seeds removed*
25g *grated tasty Cheddar cheese*

Place coarsely cut tomatoes, onion and garlic with salt and pepper in food processor, and blend until vegetables are finely chopped. Transfer this mixture to a sieve and allow excess juice to drain off. Place bread and butter in rinsed food processor and blend to yield buttered bread crumbs.

Put the hollowed-out half marrow in a large baking dish which has a small amount of water covering the bottom. Spoon tomato and onion mix evenly along hollow. Sprinkle buttered breadcrumbs, followed by grated cheese, evenly over the top. Bake at 180°C (350°F) until the marrow is cooked through. This usually takes about 50 minutes, but does vary depending on the size of the marrow. Serve hot.

*Makes 6 servings*

*Each serving provides approximately:*
**1 CARBOHYDRATE CHOICE, ½ PROTEIN CHOICE, ½ FAT & OIL CHOICE,**
**7.5g carbohydrate, 3g protein, 4g fat, 1.5g dietary fibre, 80 kcal (330 kJ)**

# Minted Tomato Salad

**Dairy free**

## Dressing
2 *tablespoons salad oil*
2 *tablespoons white vinegar*
1 *tablespoon chopped mint*
1 *clove garlic, crushed*

## Salad
*500g small tomatoes, quartered*

Place all dressing ingredients in a jar. Shake well to combine. Add to tomatoes and toss just before serving.

---

*Makes 6 servings*

*Each serving provides approximately:*
**1 FAT & OIL CHOICE,**
**2.5g carbohydrate, 0.8g protein, 4.5g fat, 1.5g dietary fibre, 55 kcal (230 kJ)**

**VARIATION:**
*Partially substitute tomatoes with peas, cucumber and/or whole-kernel corn.*

---

# Lettuce and Orange Salad

**Dairy free**

A simple salad that is very visually appealing as well as being great eating.

### Orange Dressing
3 *tablespoons olive oil (or other salad oil)*
3 *tablespoons orange juice*
*few grains cayenne pepper*

### Salad
1 *lettuce, washed*
2 *oranges, pith and rind removed, finely sliced*
6 *spring onions, chopped*
1 *green pepper, chopped into fine strips*

Place all dressing ingredients in a screw-top jar, put top on securely, then shake well to combine.

Use lettuce leaves whole, or if very large shred roughly into crisp chunky pieces. Place all the salad ingredients in a bowl, pour over dressing, then toss salad to mix and serve.

*Makes **8** servings*

*Each serving provides approximately:*
½ **CARBOHYDRATE CHOICE, 1 FAT & OIL CHOICE,**
**4.5g *carbohydrate*, 0.8g *protein*, 5g *fat*, 1.5g *dietary fibre*, 67 *kcal*
(280 *kJ*)**

**HIGH-FRUIT RECIPE**

# Jellied Beetroot

**Dairy free**

Beetroot always adds colour to a meal, but it is particularly stunning when jellied.

4 medium beetroot, washed, topped and tailed
water to cover
¼ teaspoon salt
1½ teaspoons gelatine
⅓ cup malt vinegar
2 sachets aspartame sweetener (equivalent to 4 teaspoons sugar)

Place beetroot in a saucepan, cover with water and add salt. Bring to the boil, then simmer until beetroot cooked through (about 20 minutes). Remove from heat and allow to cool. Drain cooking liquor into another container. Peel cooked beetroot and slice thinly. Place slices of beetroot in a serving dish. Return ¾ cup of cooking liquor (if there is not enough, make up to ¾ cup with water) to rinsed saucepan. Sprinkle gelatine over surface of liquor, allow to hydrate for about 5 minutes, then heat while stirring until gelatine dissolved. Add malt vinegar and sweetener, mix, then pour over sliced beetroot. Refrigerate to set.

*Makes 4 servings*

*Each serving provides approximately:*
**½ CARBOHYDRATE CHOICE,**
**6.5g carbohydrate, 2.5g protein, 3g dietary fibre, 35 kcal (150 kJ)**

# Curried Salmon and Brown Rice Salad

### Dairy free

A tasty rice salad. For best flavour prepare 4-6 hours before required.

### Curry Dressing
¼ cup olive oil (or other salad oil)
2 tablespoons lemon juice
2 tablespoons white vinegar
1 tablespoon curry powder
4 sachets aspartame sweetener (equivalent to 3 tablespoons sugar)

### Salad
1 cup brown rice
2 cups water
½ teaspoon salt
1 teaspoon vegetable oil
3 spring onions, chopped
1 stick celery, chopped
200g fresh smoked salmon, flaked (or 210g can salmon, drained and flaked)
1 tomato, finely chopped
¼ cup raisins

Place brown rice, water, salt and oil in a heavy-bottomed saucepan. Bring to the boil with the lid off, boil for 2 minutes, then turn the heat down until the water is only just simmering. Cover, and leave just simmering for 45 minutes *without stirring*. When done the rice will have absorbed all the water and will be cooked to perfection. Rinse the cooked rice under cold running water and drain well.

Place all the dressing ingredients in a screw-top jar, screw top on securely, and shake well to combine ingredients.

Combine drained cooked rice with the other salad ingredients. Pour dressing over the top, and toss salad to mix dressing through. Refrigerate salad until required, then toss again just before serving.

**Makes 8 servings**

*Each serving provides approximately:*
2½ CARBOHYDRATE CHOICES, 1 PROTEIN CHOICE, 1 FAT
& OIL CHOICE,
*26g carbohydrate, 6.5g protein, 9g fat, 1.5g dietary fibre, 210 kcal
(870 kJ)*

# Yoghurt Dressing

A quickly made, low-fat alternative for salad dressing.

*¼ teaspoon prepared mustard*
*2 teaspoons lemon juice*
*½ cup unsweetened low-fat natural yoghurt*
*freshly ground black pepper*
*1 sachet aspartame sweetener (equivalent to 2 teaspoons sugar)*

Mix prepared mustard with lemon juice, then add to yoghurt along
with the pepper and sweetener. Mix well. Keep refrigerated.

**Makes 8 servings, approximately ½ cup**

*1 serving = 1 tablespoon*
**FREE FOOD**
*1g carbohydrate, 0.7g protein, 0.2g fat, 9 kcal (38 kJ)*

# Fresh Herb Dressing

**Dairy free**

Adding fresh herbs gives extra piquancy to a vinaigrette dressing. This is a combination that I enjoy, but there are an infinite number of variations possible. Use a selection of your favourite herbs, or simply add whatever herbs you have on hand.

¼ cup olive oil (or other salad oil)
2 tablespoons lemon juice
2 tablespoons wine vinegar
¼ teaspoon prepared mustard
freshly ground black pepper
1 clove garlic, crushed
1 tablespoon finely chopped chives
1 tablespoon finely chopped parsley
½ teaspoon finely chopped onion

Place all ingredients in a screw-top jar, screw on top securely, and shake well to combine. Store in refrigerator.

---

**Makes 10 servings, approximately ⅔ cup**

**1 serving = 1 tablespoon**
**1 FAT & OIL CHOICE,**
**0.2g carbohydrate, 0.1g protein, 5.5g fat, 51 kcal (210 kJ)**

---

# FOOD CHOICES PROVIDED BY INGREDIENTS

Here is a list of FOOD CHOICES provided by ingredients commonly used in baking and desserts.

This information is provided to allow you to calculate easily the FOOD CHOICES provided by recipes you use for which no compositional data is given, as is the case with recipes in most general cookbooks.

The following approximate weights of ingredients per measure are based on using level standard metric measures lightly packed (i.e. packed without compressing ingredients down into measure used).

| MEASURE | CAPACITY |
|---|---|
| 1 level standard metric cup | 250 millilitres |
| 1 level standard metric tablespoon | 15 millilitres |
| 1 level standard metric teaspoon | 5 millilitres |

**Note:** 3 teaspoons = 1 tablespoon
There are approximately 4 tablespoons in ¼ cup, and approximately 16 tablespoons in 1 cup.

The FOOD CHOICE values given are based on the FOOD CHOICE Plan used at Waikato Hospital:

- 1 CARBOHYDRATE CHOICE (abbreviated as C) contains approximately 10g carbohydrate.
- 1 PROTEIN CHOICE (abbreviated as P) contains approximately 7g protein and 5g fat.
- 1 FAT & OIL CHOICE (abbreviated as F) contains approximately 5g of fat.

| | Measure | Approximate Weight | Approximate FOOD CHOICES Provided |
|---|---|---|---|
| **Cereals and Cereal Products:** | | | |
| Flour (unsifted) | 1 tablespoon | 9g | ½ C |
| | 1 cup | 150g | 10 C |
| Wholemeal flour | 1 tablespoon | 9g | ½ C |
| | 1 cup | 150g | 10 C |
| Rye flour | 1 tablespoon | 8g | ½ C |
| | 1 cup | 130g | 10 C |
| Cornflour, custard powder, arrowroot | 1 tablespoon | 8g | ½ C |
| | 1 cup | 135g | 12½ C |
| Ground Rice | 1 tablespoon | 10g | 1 C |
| | 1 cup | 160g | 13 C |
| Rolled oats | 1 cup | 90g | 5½ C |
| Oatmeal (fine) | 1 cup | 140g | 9½ C |
| Wheatgerm | 1 cup | 80g | 3½ C, 2 P |
| Bran flakes | 1 cup | 45g | 1 C, 1 P |
| Wholegrain bread | 1 medium slice | 25g | 1 C |
| Wholegrain breadcrumbs (soft, lightly packed) | 1 cup | 60g | 2 C |
| Dry breadcrumbs | 1 cup | 115g | 9 C |
| Wine biscuits | 250g pack (approx. 40 biscuits) | 250g | 20 C |
| Long grain rice, short grain rice, brown rice (uncooked) | 1 cup | 200g | 17 C |
| Sago (uncooked) | 1 cup | 180g | 17 C |
| Cornflakes | 1 cup | 30g | 2½ C |
| Rice bubbles | 1 cup | 30g | 2½ C |

| | Measure | Approximate Weight | Approximate FOOD CHOICES Provided |
|---|---|---|---|
| **Fruit and Fruit Juices:** | | | |
| *Lemon juice | 1 cup | 250g | ½ C |
| *Other fruit juices | 1 cup | 250g | 2½ C |
| **Stewed and canned fruits (all varieties) | 1 cup | 260g | 2½ C |
| Mashed banana | 1 cup | 250g | 5 C |
| Grated apple (lightly packed) | 1 cup | 100g | 1 C |
| Sultanas, raisins | 1 cup | 155g | 10 C |
| Currants | 1 cup | 130g | 8 C |
| Dried apricot halves (unchopped) | 4 halves | 20g | 1 C |
| | 1 cup | 120g | 5 C |
| Pitted dates (unchopped) | 3 dates | 18g | 1 C |
| | 1 cup | 160g | 10 C |
| Pitted prunes (unchopped) | 2 prunes | 24g | 1 C |
| | 1 cup | 170g | 7 C |

\* Unsweetened or artificially sweetened, i.e. no added sugar
\** Stewed or canned in water or fruit juice with no added sugar

**Note:** 1 lemon provides approximately 2 tablespoons lemon juice
1 orange provides approximately ¼ cup orange juice
1 grapefruit provides approximately ⅓ cup grapefruit juice
2 large bananas or 3 medium bananas yield approximately 1 cup of mashed banana.

| | Measure | Approximate Weight | Approximate FOOD CHOICES Provided |
|---|---|---|---|
| **Vegetables:** | | | |
| Grated carrot (lightly packed) | 1 cup | 90g | ½ C |
| Pumpkin (cooked, drained and mashed) | 1 cup | 250g | 1 C |

**Note:** Non-starchy (or non-complex carbohydrate) vegetables are FREE FOODS, e.g. tomatoes, onions and courgettes.

| | Measure | Approximate Weight | Approximate FOOD CHOICES Provided |
|---|---|---|---|
| **Dairy Products:** | | | |
| Trim milk | 1 cup | 250g | 1½ C, 1½ P |
| Instant non-fat milk powder | 1 cup | 110g | 5½ C, 6 P |
| Low-fat cottage cheese | 1 cup | 250g | 5½ P |
| Low-fat soft cheese | 1 cup | 300g | 3½ C, 4 P |
| Low-fat sour cream | 1 cup | 250g | 6 F |
| UHT evaporated milk | 1 cup | 265g | 2½ C, 3 P |
| Unsweetened low-fat natural yoghurt | 1 cup | 255g | 1½ C, 1½ P |
| UHT low-fat cream | 1 cup | 250g | 6 F |
| Cream | 1 cup | 245g | 19½ F |
| Cream cheese | 1 cup | 250g | 17 F |
| Grated Cheddar cheese (lightly packed) | 1 cup | 80g | 3 P, 2½ F |

| | Measure | Approximate Weight | Approximate FOOD CHOICES Provided |
|---|---|---|---|
| **Eggs:** | | | |
| Egg | 1 x No. 6 | 55g | 1 P |
| Egg yolk | from 1 x No. 6 | 20g | ½P, ½F |
| Egg white | from 1 x No. 6 | 35g | ½ P |

| | Measure | Approximate Weight | Approximate FOOD CHOICES Provided |
|---|---|---|---|
| **Nuts and Seeds:** | | | |
| Desiccated coconut | 1 cup | 70g | 8½ F |
| Peanuts | 1 cup | 155g | 15 F |
| Walnut halves | 4 halves | 10g | 1 F |
| Walnut pieces | 1 cup | 100g | 10 F |
| Almonds, blanched whole | 10 almonds | 10g | 1 F |
| | 1 cup | 160g | 17 F |
| Sunflower seeds | 1 cup | 140g | 14 F |
| Pumpkin seeds | 1 cup | 140g | 13 F |
| Sesame seeds | 1 cup | 150g | 15 F |
| Peanut butter | 1 cup | 270g | 29 F |
| Ground almonds | 1 tablespoon | 6g | ½ F |
| | 1 cup | 100g | 10½ F |

| | Measure | Approximate Weight | Approximate FOOD CHOICES Provided |
|---|---|---|---|
| **Fats and Oils:** | | | |
| Butter, margarine | 1 tablespoon | 15g | 2½ F |
| | 1 cup | 250g | 41 F |
| Vegetable oil, vegetable shortening | 1 tablespoon | 14g | 3 F |
| (melted) | 1 cup | 225g | 45 F |

| | Measure | Approximate Weight | Approximate FOOD CHOICES Provided |
|---|---|---|---|
| ***Sugar and Sugar Products:** | | | |
| White sugar | 1 tablespoon | 15g | 1½ C |
| Brown sugar | 1 tablespoon | 10g | 1 C |
| Icing sugar | 1 tablespoon | 10g | 1 C |
| Golden syrup | 1 tablespoon | 20g | 1½ C |
| Honey | 1 tablespoon | 20g | 1½ C |

* Only acceptable for use in small quantities (less than ½ teaspoon per serving).

| | Measure | Approximate Weight | Approximate FOOD CHOICES Provided |
|---|---|---|---|
| **Miscellaneous:** | | | |
| Cocoa | 1 tablespoon | 6g | FREE |
| | 1 cup | 100g | 2½ P, 2 F |
| Carob powder | 1 tablespoon | 6g | ½ C |
| | 1 cup | 100g | 7½ C |
| Gelatine | 1 tablespoon | 10g | 1 P |
| Bacon (lean) | 1 rasher | 50g | 1 P |

## Calculating FOOD CHOICES for Recipes

Do not bother to calculate to one or more decimal places, just round off to the nearest ½ CHOICE for each ingredient or serving. Calculating to 'x' decimal places gives more accurate looking figures but this appearance is deceiving. Ingredients do not have a constant composition, but vary from one source of supply to another, and from one growing season to the next. The preceding FOOD CHOICES listed for each ingredient are themselves approximate, not precise. Do not try to create a degree of accuracy which does not exist.

Disregard minor ingredients like bicarbonate of soda, baking powder, spices and other seasonings. These make no significant contribution to the FOOD CHOICES provided by the total recipe.

Unless volumes of a tablespoon or less are involved, work from the information provided for cup measures. It is more accurate to use base data for larger measures, because the smaller the measure the greater the rounding off errors involved in the FOOD CHOICE values calculated.

*Measure ingredient quantities and serving sizes with reasonable care, or the* FOOD CHOICES *calculated for a serving of a recipe will bear little relevance to what is actually eaten.* For greater accuracy weigh ingredients in preference to measuring by volume, especially where large quantities are involved. Examples of FOOD CHOICE calculations for recipes are included in the next section.

# TIPS ON MODIFYING 'NON-DIABETIC' RECIPES

Recipes that are high in sugar and/or fat are not suitable for diabetics. Many high-sugar recipes can simply have sugar deleted, or replaced with an appropriate quantity of artificial sweetener, to produce very acceptable results. Most drinks and low-fat dessert recipes (jellies, custards, milk puddings, etc.) come into this category. However in other recipes, in particular for baked goods, both sugar and fat have a marked influence on the texture of the end product. There are no hard and fast rules which will produce guaranteed success when modifying these recipes, but here are some general guidelines.

1. Select recipes which can be made easily without added sugar; avoid recipes which involve creaming butter and sugar, or caramelisation of sugar.
2. Look at the fat content of a selected recipe. Try to keep this to 1 FAT & OIL CHOICE per serving or less. For biscuits, cakes and slices, fat can usually be reduced successfully to this level. However, this goal is unrealistic for some types of recipes, for example those which involve pastry (such recipes should not be used frequently).
3. Consider if sugar is important for crispness or flavour of the product. It is best to retain a little sugar in biscuit recipes for crispness. Bran muffins without a little golden syrup for flavouring are not very palatable. If you decide to retain some sugar, golden syrup or honey in a recipe, keep it to less than ½ teaspoon per serving.
4. Delete any salt included. Very few baking or dessert recipes require salt to be added to achieve an acceptable flavour – there are some exceptions (for example, some savoury and bread recipes) but not very many.
5. For recipes that have significant amounts of sugar and/or fat deleted, increase the amount of moisture added — add extra water, Trim milk, fruit juice, fruit pulp or yoghurt – unsweetened of course. Both sugar and fat contribute to the perceived moistness of baked goods, and their removal produces a drier product unless some compensation is made. How much extra

moistness is required varies greatly – add a little extra, say 2 tablespoons to ¼ cup, and judge from the consistency of the mixture as to whether you should add any more.

6. Remember that when you delete large quantities of sugar and/or fat from a recipe you are reducing the total bulk of the recipe (extra moistness added does not usually compensate for the total bulk removed). Sometimes it is desirable to increase the total bulk of the recipe, (for example for slices) so you do not end up with a thin, meagre-looking product.

7. Use wholemeal flour as much as possible. Often replacing all the flour in a recipe with wholemeal flour can give a very crumbly end result, but half-and-half wholemeal and plain flour usually gives very acceptable results. Increased use of wholemeal flour can lead to a drier product too. This can be another reason for adding extra moisture.

8. If necessary add artificial sweetener. For recipes where you can check the sweetness level during preparation, just add sweetener gradually until an acceptable level is obtained. For baked recipes this is not always so easy. As a starting point add sufficient liquid artificial sweetener to provide sweetness equivalent to two thirds of the sugar deleted, less still if a significant quantity of dried fruit (or other sweet tasting fruit or fruit juice) is included in the recipe. Each time you make a recipe, reduce the amount of sweetener added until you find the minimum level acceptable to you and your family.

9. If you do try to modify a recipe that involves creaming of butter and sugar make the recipe by either:
   • rubbing the butter through the dry ingredients first, then adding the liquid ingredients (including liquid artificial sweetener if used); or
   • melting the butter (or substituting vegetable oil for butter) and mixing all the ingredients together in one step.

   When butter and sugar are creamed together air is incorporated into the mixture which expands during baking and helps leaven the product. To compensate for the omission of this mixing step, add extra baking powder and/or bicarbonate of soda, to about one and a half times that in the original recipe.

It is great fun experimenting with recipes and very satisfying when you come up with a new 'hit' recipe. The more you experiment the greater your success rate will be as you gain more of a feel for what you are doing. Do expect some failures – we all have them. Here are two examples of 'non-diabetic' recipes I have modified to be suitable for diabetics. I hope they will help you on your way to trying some new recipes of your own.

# Example 1: Dusky Dandy

*Original recipe — unsuitable for diabetics*

| Ingredients | Approximate FOOD CHOICES Provided | | |
|---|---|---|---|
| | CARBOHYDRATE CHOICES | PROTEIN CHOICES | FAT & OIL CHOICES |
| 120g butter | — | — | 19½ |
| ½ cup coconut, toasted | — | — | 4½ |
| 1 cup sultanas | 10 | — | — |
| 1 cup flour | 10 | — | — |
| 1 teaspoon baking powder | — | — | — |
| 1 tablespoon cocoa | — | — | — |
| ¾ cup sugar | 19 | — | — |
| ½ teaspoon vanilla essence | — | — | — |
| 1 egg | — | 1 | — |
| | 39 | 1 | 24 |

**METHOD**

Mix all ingredients together. Spread evenly into greased sponge roll tin. Bake 20 minutes at 180°C (350°F). When cool, ice with chocolate icing and sprinkle coconut over the surface. Cut into 24 fingers or squares.

I am sure many of you have made a chocolate square recipe similar to this. If you simply strip off the icing, and use liquid artificial sweetener instead of sugar in the base, a thin dry crumbly product results.

The following modifications yield a very acceptable product:
1. Doubling the recipe. This gives more depth to the square.
2. Reducing the fat. Doubling the recipe brings the total number of FAT & OIL CHOICES to 48, or 2 per serving, which is much

higher than desired. In a square recipe this size I have found an acceptable product can be obtained using 100g butter.

3. Deleting sugar and adding liquid artificial sweetener to provide sweetness. As the cocoa and coconut flavours predominate no sugar needs to be added for flavouring. The double recipe would have contained 1½ cups of sugar, but 2 tablespoons of liquid artificial sweetener (equivalent to 1 cup of sugar) more than suffices.
4. Replacing half of the flour with wholemeal flour.
5. Adding extra liquid. With the deletion of sugar, reduction of fat, and inclusion of some wholemeal flour, extra liquid is required to achieve acceptable moistness in the baked square. Half a cup of Trim milk provides this.

### *Modified recipe — suitable for diabetics*

| Ingredients | Approximate FOOD CHOICES Provided | | |
|---|---|---|---|
| | CARBOHYDRATE CHOICES | PROTEIN CHOICES | FAT & OIL CHOICES |
| 100g butter, melted | — | — | 16½ |
| 1 cup coconut, toasted | — | — | 8½ |
| 2 cups sultanas | 20 | — | — |
| 1 cup flour | 10 | — | — |
| 1 cup wholemeal flour | 10 | — | — |
| 2 teaspoons baking powder | — | — | — |
| 2 tablespoons cocoa | — | ½ | — |
| 2 tablespoons liquid   artificial sweetener | — | — | — |
| ½ cup Trim milk | 1 | 1 | — |
| 1 teaspoon vanilla essence | — | — | — |
| 2 eggs | — | 2 | — |
| | 41 | 3½ | 25 |
| Divided into 24 servings = per serving | 1½ | — | 1 |

**Each serving provides approximately: 1½ CARBOHYDRATE CHOICES and 1 FAT & OIL CHOICE**

As approximately half of the total CARBOHYDRATE CHOICES in the recipe (20 out of 41) come from fruit, in this case sultanas, this recipe comes into the HIGH-FRUIT category.

It is interesting to note that doubling the recipe, with the modifications listed, does not significantly alter the total FOOD CHOICES provided. The calories provided per serving of the modified recipe are therefore approximately the same as in the original recipe (un-iced), despite it being nearly double in bulk.

This recipe is included in the *Biscuits and Slices* section (see p. 54).

# Example 2: Fruity Muffins

*Original recipe — unsuitable for diabetics*

| Ingredients | Approximate FOOD CHOICES Provided | | |
|---|---|---|---|
| | CARBOHYDRATE CHOICES | PROTEIN CHOICES | FAT & OIL CHOICES |
| 1½ cups flour (sifted, 190g) | 12½ | — | — |
| 2 teaspoons mixed spice | — | — | — |
| 2 teaspoons bicarbonate of soda | — | — | — |
| ¼ teaspoon salt | — | — | — |
| ⅓ cup sugar | 8½ | — | — |
| ½ cup sultanas | 5 | — | — |
| 1 egg, beaten | — | 1 | — |
| ¾ cup stewed apples, peaches, crushed pineapple or other fruit | 2 | — | — |
| 50g butter, melted | — | — | 8 |
| | 28 | 1 | 8 |

## METHOD

Sift flour, measure, then sift again with other dry ingredients (except sugar). Stir in sugar and sultanas. Add beaten egg, fruit (mashed if necessary) and melted butter, without stirring between additions. Mix just enough to combine. Spoon mixture into 12 greased patty pans. Bake for 10-15 minutes at 200°C (400°F).

Looking at this recipe, each muffin provides approximtely ½ FAT & OIL CHOICE, which is quite acceptable. So the only essential change required is to cut the sugar down. Apart from providing sweetness the sugar is not important for flavour – the mixed spice and fruit added are the key flavour ingredients – so the sugar can be deleted altogether.

Changing the recipe as follows produces delicious muffins with no added sugar:

1. Deleting the sugar and salt.
2. Replacing 1½ cups of sifted flour with ¾ cup wholemeal flour and ½ cup of flour (both unsifted). I do not sift flour before I measure it (using predominantly wholemeal flour, and food processor mixing, I have got out of the habit). Sifted flour takes up a greater volume, because of the air incorporated, than unsifted flour. Hence the reduction in total flour from 1½ cups to 1¼ cups. To incorporate air into the mixture, stir the dry ingredients with a fork before adding sultanas.
3. Opting to use crushed pineapple (the undrained contents of a 230g can) as fruit, because of the choices, given this has the most natural sweetness. With the sweetness from this pineapple, plus that from the sultanas, the muffins are quite sweet enough without any artificial sweetener added. The 230g crushed pineapple is closer to a cup than ¾ cup of fruit, providing extra moisture to compensate for the sugar omitted.

### Modified recipe — suitable for diabetics

| Ingredients | Approximate FOOD CHOICES Provided | | |
| --- | --- | --- | --- |
| | CARBOHYDRATE CHOICES | PROTEIN CHOICES | FAT & OIL CHOICES |
| ¾ cup wholemeal flour | 7½ | — | — |
| ½ cup flour | 5 | — | — |
| 2 teaspoons mixed spice | — | — | — |
| 1 teaspoon bicarbonate of soda | — | — | — |
| ½ cup sultanas | 5 | — | — |
| 1 egg, beaten | — | 1 | — |
| 230g can of crushed pineapple, undrained (¾-1 cup) | 2½ | — | — |
| 50g butter, melted | — | — | 8 |
| | 20 | 1 | 8 |
| Divided into 12 muffins = per muffin | 1½ | — | ½ |

**Each muffin provides approximately: 1½ CARBOHYDRATE CHOICES, ½ FAT & OIL CHOICE**

The CARBOHYDRATE CHOICES provided by the fruit in this recipe (the sultanas and pineapple) make up only 7½ out of the total of 20 (38%), so it is not a HIGH-FRUIT recipe.

This Fruity Muffin recipe can be found in the *Scones and Muffins* section (see p. 45).

*Note: The* FAT & OIL CHOICES *per serving differ slightly –* 1 FAT & OIL CHOICE *per serving when calculated from food composition tables versus* ½ FAT & OIL CHOICE *per serving obtained using the simplified* FOOD CHOICE *system. This is because only the predominant* FOOD CHOICES *provided by each ingredient are included in the simplified* FOOD CHOICE *system. As carbohydrate is the predominant component in most baked goods, the protein and fat contents are often underestimated.*

As I said earlier, do not try and create a degree of accuracy which does not exist. For good diabetic control, reasonable care with recipe preparation, portion sizes, and overall meal planning will provide approximately the FOOD CHOICES required. Do not get tied in knots with pedantic measurements and calculations. *Keep it simple and stick with it.*

# INDEX

Ambrosia with Oranges  82
Apple Cream Pie  110
Apple Honey Slice  58
Apple Prune Pie  108
Apple Shortcake  107
Apricot and Pineapple
  Shortcake  106
Apricot and Pineapple
  Spread  32
Apricot Brandy Ice-Cream  113
Apricot Sponge Pudding  96

Banana Smoothie  29
Banana Yoghurt Loaf  61
Banana Yoghurt Slice  79
Banana, Orange and Coconut
  Loaf  62
Berry Ice-Cream  113
Berry Yoghurt Jelly  81
Blueberry Tart  94
Boysenberry Crush  73

Carob Orange Square  56
Cassata  114
Celebration Cake  70
Cheese Spread  36
Chicken Liver Pâté  38
Chocolate  131
Chocolate Cake  67
Chocolate Crackles  120
Chocolate Custard  100
Chocolate Fudge Cake  134
Chocolate Ice-Cream  113
Chocolate Mousse  84
Chocolate Sauce  101
Chocolate Smoothie  28
Chocolate Steamed Pudding  97
Chocolate Yoghurt Glaze  127
Christmas Cake  138
Christmas Pudding  144
Citrus Supreme Cheesecake  116
Coffee Creams  89
Coffee Walnut Ice-Cream  113

Courgette and Carrot Muffins  46
Courgette Slice  150
Creamy Rice Pudding  85
Curried Salmon and
  Brown Rice Salad  156
Curry Beansprout Muffins  48
**Custards**
  Chocolate Custard  100
  Orange Brandy Custard  137
  Vanilla Custard  99

Date and Orange Shortcake  107
Date and Orange Spread  33
Date and Wheatgerm Scones  42
**Drinks**
  Banana Smoothie  29
  Chocolate Smoothie  28
  Grapefruit Cordial  24
  Harvest Drink  25
  King's Cup  26
  Lemon Cordial  23
  Mint Julep  28
  Orange and Lemon Cordial  24
  Party Punch  27
Dusky Dandy  54

Easter Nests  148

Fresh Apricot Cheesecake  105
Fresh Herb Dressing  158
Frozen Tropical Sherbet  76
Fruit and Tea Loaf  63
Fruit Mince Slice  142
Fruity Muffins  45

Gingerbread Loaf  64
Gingerbread Men  118
**Glazes and Toppings for Cakes**
  Chocolate Yoghurt Glaze  127
  Lemon Soft-Cheese Glaze  129
  Nutty Carob Topping  126
  Vanilla Soft-Cheese Glaze  128
Grapefruit Cordial  24

Harvest Drink   25
Herb Pumpkin Damper   44
Hot Cross Buns   146

Ice-Cream   112
Ice-Cream Pudding   88

Jaffa Balls   132
Jellied Beetroot   155

King's Cup   26

Lemon and Sultana Rice
   Pudding   86
Lemon Apple Spread   31
Lemon Bliss   78
Lemon Cheese Pudding   87
Lemon Cordial   23
Lemon Sauce   102
Lemon Soft-Cheese Glaze   129
Lettuce and Orange Salad   154
Light Cream Filling   129

Mint Julep      28
Minted Sorbet   74
Minted Tomato Salad   153

Nut and Raisin Chocolate   130
Nutty Carob Balls   133
Nutty Carob Topping   126

Orange and Lemon Cordial   24
Orange Boats   124
Orange Brandy Custard   137
Orange Custard Pie   95
Orange Peanut Cake   69

Party Punch   27
Peaches and Cream Muffins   46
Peanut Brownies   52
Pears in Lemon Jelly   80
Pineapple Fruit Cake   71
Pizza Faces   122
Pumpkin Pie   93

Quick Mix Christmas Cake   140

Rolled Oat and Coconut
   Biscuits   51
Rolled Oat Pie Base   92

Sago Plum Pudding   98
**Salad Dressings**
   Fresh Herb Dressing   158
   Yoghurt Dressing   157

**Salads**
   Curried Salmon and
      Brown Rice Salad   156
   Lettuce and Orange Salad   154
   Minted Tomato Salad   153
Salmon and Egg Spread   36
**Sauces**
   Chocolate Sauce   101
   Lemon Sauce   102
   Spicy Orange Sauce   103
Savoury Scones   41
Shortbread Triangles   53
Smoked Mussel Pâté   38
Spanish Cream   90
Spice Biscuits   50
Spicy Carrot Cake   68
Spicy Orange Sauce   103
Spicy Sultana and
   Apricot Scones   43
Spinach Slice   151
**Spreads**
   Apricot and Pineapple
      Spread   32
   Cheese Spread   36
   Chicken Liver Pâté   38
   Date and Orange Spread   33
   Lemon Apple Spread   31
   Salmon and Egg Spread   36
   Smoked Mussel Pâté   38
   Strawberry Spread   34
   Three Fruit Marmalade   34
Strawberry Marshmallow
   Shortcake   120

Strawberry Mousse  83
Strawberry Spread  34
Strawberry Water Ice  75

Three Fruit Marmalade  34
Toasted Cheese Rolls  37
Tomato and Onion Stuffed
  Marrow  152

Vanilla Custard  99
Vanilla Soft-Cheese Glaze  128

**Vegetable Dishes**
  Courgette Slice  150
  Jellied Beetroot  155
  Spinach Slice  151

White Christmas  136
Wholemeal Banana Cake  66

Yoghurt Dressing  157